I0179017

Soul On Empty

A Journey of the Soul

Soul On Empty
A Journey of the Soul

Toni Holmes

Dumouriez Publishing
Jacksonville, Florida

SOUL ON EMPTY- A Journey of the Soul

Unless otherwise indicated, all scripture quotations and references are from the King James Version of the Bible.

To contact the author or to get inforomation for appearances or speaking engagements visit or send inquiries to toniholmesthebookwriter@gmail.com ; www.myspace.com/soulonempty1

Copyright © 2008
Toni Holmes
All rights reserved.

This copyright covers materials written expressly for this volume. Reproduction or transmission by any means, electronic or mechanical, including photocopying and recording, or by information storage or retrieval system, with the exception of brief quotations in reviews or articles must be arranged with the individual copyright holder.

Published by:
Dumouriez Publishing
P.O.Box 12849
Jacksonville, Florida 32209
http//www.dpublishing1.com

ISBN: 0-9764387-5-5   ISBN 13: 978-0-9764387-5-5
Printed in the United States of America.

I dedicate this book to those who have not yet found their voice. The Children of Promise Located at 600 Lafayette Avenue, 6th Floor, Brooklyn, New York 11216 (718) 483-9290. To any organization, that is embracing and empowering children of incarcerated parents. Thank you Master Prophet E. Bernard Jordan for helping me to find my voice.

Acknowledgements

I would like to acknowledge my mother, Mary Holmes who is the strongest women I know…I adore you. My Father, William Holmes who *Reached* and found there was something there…Miss you. My Siblings, Gary, Marsette, and Celeste, "Thank you for all of the love."

My Friends, Andrea, Sheila, Elaine, Bob, and Cynthia, "You are God's Gifts to me." My granddaughters, Sheyenne and Kailyn Randolph who reminds me how important it is for parents and children to know each other.

I truly thank the various Sponsors that helped to breathe life into this work so that it can be a help to others and The Company of Prophets who Hid me until the appointed time…

Contents

Dedication
Acknowledgements
Preface

Chapter 1:	I Wanna Tell You Something	15
Chapter 2:	I Come From A Dry Place	21
Chapter 3:	The Need To Be Free	35
Chapter 4:	Get A Life	39
Chapter 5:	Who Will Roll Away The Stone	55
Chapter 6:	In My Mind	75
Chapter 7:	Passion For A New Possibility	83
Chapter 8:	Time	93
Chapter 9:	Calm Trust	97

Chapter 10:	Dip Deeply	103
Chapter 11:	Garden of Eden	111
Chapter 12:	Crucible	117
Appendix		123
About the Author		141

Preface

What keeps you from facing issues is…

Denial, Denial, Denial
Denial isn't just a River in Egypt

As long as there is, breath in the body the opportunity is always there for change. No matter how good or bad one's life is, a challenge shall present itself (this is necessary it's called choice and growth). Handling the challenges has been part of the "Issues of life." Some issues go deep but those with no coping skills and no fight for a challenge or those with deep guilt usually turn away or ignore. Oftentimes, they think this is coping.

To those who cannot express what they feel there is depression. For those who look outward, there is almost always disappointment (Drinking and drugs). Eventually life is not lived. Even though this state of mind is present, it is not concrete. The challenge to "Want To Live" is the issue at hand. It is not as easy as it seems to give up. You work at convincing yourself that the light at the end of the tunnel is a train.

The one who gives up usually struggles with this for a while before they let go. By the time others see an empty soul, it has become reserved for something greater than anything you or I could give. One must reach bottom to get to the deep well. If anyone wants to help then light the way. If you want to make someone thirsty, be the salt of the earth.

Trust usually has to be rebuilt but by this time, bridges are usually no longer there. Don't become disappointed when the results are not instant because a home can't be built in a day. It has never been the plan for "any" man to walk alone. Seeking and Knocking is the requirement of the soul on empty…and you shall find.

Chapter One

I WANNA TELL YOU SOMETHING

What is a Soul on Empty? Could it be you? Perhaps, someone you know? Or someone you may be passing everyday? The first encounter I had with a soul on empty was my father. It was because of him that I reached beyond my own ability to see a life transformed. I've come to understand that this can only be done by the renewing of the mind.

Take this journey with me and you will see an unfolding—As deep calleth unto deep you shall hear the words that Jesus spoke to the deaf and mute man when he took him aside from the multitude and said "Ephphatha" *Be opened.* *(Mark 7:34)* Which means, you are no longer sealed or tied. On this journey, it will become almost impossible to keep it to yourself. A part of you shall begin to hear and your tongue shall be loosed, to tell your own story.

At the age of seven, I can remember wondering where my father was. I wasn't allowed to see him, and it was getting harder all the time. I remembered his smile, his eyes, and the smell of violet on his breath...And most of all his promises. I think I held on to them like a drop of crazy glue on the wrong thing. I could recall all of this as a young child, and then all of a sudden he was no more...My heart began to miss him.

Even as a child, it was abnormal for me not to have a family. Families were everywhere, the church, the school, and the neighborhood. Why was I born in a dysfunctional family? It was starting to become an issue for me. My mother really couldn't make any more excuses for my father. My mom was determined to move on.

It took strength courage and guts. Yes, it was his problem, but what about me? Eventually, my mother had to tell me that my father was in prison. She had divorced him and was remarried by this time. I know now that her intention was to protect my brother, my sister, and myself. She felt that keeping our father out of our lives would make our lives better.

Why can't I let go? There was something that felt empty in me that I couldn't explain. It was a feeling, ever pulling me closer to him. Even at that age, I knew I was on a path that would not let me go. I wanted my mom to find out how I could get in contact with him, but I could tell that it was ripping her heart out.

Little did I know about the thin line between love and disappointment. I think I was becoming a disappointment to her, by my behavior but I was living on fading memories. I guess I was too young to handle the truth, but as time went on, things changed.

Tension around the house was mounting because I was so uncooperative with Gary, my boneheaded brother. He and I were always getting into it, (My fault, I guess☺). Even though he was 4 years older, I picked on him because he was always telling me what to do. I hated that because he would never do what he was supposed to do.

When he was told to do something, he made me do it. Especially because he was warned not to pick at me but always did. He would tell me my teeth were too big or that someone left me on the doorstep and if it weren't for him, I'd still be out there. Stuff like that kept me going. I always wanted to go with him wherever he went. "He's a boy," mom would say. Who cared? I was trying to make his life miserable.

One day Gary was listening in on one of my mother's phone calls. I told him if he didn't tell me, what the conversation was about I was going to tell. I said that yelling at the top of my voice. Well you would have thought I said something bad. We started fighting and he was trying to keep me from hitting him.

The turning point for us came on a day that my mother went next door for half an hour. By the time she got back, I was under the kitchen table hiding. My mom came in and started hollering, "Toni, why are you under that table?"

I simply said, "Gary is mad because he thought I was going to tell on him but I really don't know anything."

My mom yelled, "You stop running your mouth Toni and Gary you'd better stop picking at her; you should be protecting her." Mom failed to mention no bumps on the head.

He would always reply, "She doesn't need protection, I do." After that, my brother and I never fought again.

There were three of us at that time and we were all four years apart, Gary, Marsette, and I. My mother was trying to make things work and I was messing things up. We had moved to a new neighborhood in East Orange, New Jersey after she had gotten remarried. That meant a new school for me and I hated that. This time I acted out. You know how the first day of school is. What did you do over the summer?

Where did your family go on vacation? That question sent me to the moon, because most of the people I knew didn't go on vacations, they just went south. Over the summer, we stayed up late and played tag or dodge ball in the streets. We usually went in the house way after the street lights came on. We even went to our country cousin's house, (Fanny Mae and Huey), for a cookout. Some of you know what I'm talking about 'cause most of us have country cousins.

On this particular day, the first day of school, it was time for introductions. I was new at the school so no one knew me at all. Good! "Now's my time to escape," I thought. It was my turn to stand and introduce myself. The teacher said, "And what's your name?"

I said, "Tonya Dalton." Now my name was Toni Holmes when I left for school that morning. My mother had remarried and that was her new last name. Dalton that meant I was disconnected from her as well as my father. Tonya was just a name I made up out of the blue. What were they trying to do to me? Between that, the tooth fairy, Santa and the Easter Bunny, I thought I was nuts.

I didn't want to be real either I wanted to disappear. The teacher looked at the paper and then looked at me. By looking at the paper, she knew exactly what my name was but she just left it alone and probably thought she needed to speak with my mother and that she did. She called my mother that night and I heard about it. The teacher and my mom worked something out.

Chapter Two

I COME FROM A DRY PLACE

My father often rehearsed that he was the sixth of seven children, (as if that would explain why he was the way, he was). There were five boys and two girls (Maurice, Brewster, Otis, Margaret, Lloyd, William, and Roberta). Maurice was the brother everybody looked up to. He was the responsible one and had always tried to take care of his mother and siblings. He was charming and he was a big time gambler whose life ended tragically.

Brewster was the tough one. Otis was a professional boxer. Maurice made him get involved with that because he was so angry. Maurice thought that boxing would help him release some energy and it did. Lloyd was always well behaved because he didn't want to be like anyone else but his older brother. Margaret was the oldest girl and she became an introvert, and her mother made her that way.

My father, William, was a singer, a ladies–man, a charmer and the most easily influenced. Roberta was the baby and she had been spoiled by everyone. She and Margaret were protected by their crazy brothers, which meant dating was impossible for them. Their looks caused a lot of trouble. They might have been the only teen-aged girls in town with no boyfriend. Because of their five brothers, no one was willing to step up to the plate. The Holmes brothers had everything but key ingredients. There was something missing. No substance and no character, so crumbling was inevitable.

One night changed my father forever. It was 1948, the same year that he and my mom met. At that time he was singing in a ballroom where the big bands played--Billy Eckstein, Sarah Vaughn, Lionel Hampton, Billy Holiday, Count Basie, and Joe Williams to name a few. Anyway, they were all there at some point and time they would ask my father to sing with them when they were in town, and introduced him as a local. From what I heard, this joint was jumpin' and it was right on Belmont Avenue in Newark, New Jersey.

My mom along with her friends Rosetta, Daisy, Gloria, and Gladys were out on the town and looking good that night. My mother, as she recalls, had on a flare dress that she said was made just for dancing. The top of the dress had a black scoop neck with rhinestones around the collar and the bottom was black with a lot of movement when she danced.

During that, time women wore very high-heeled shoes. I really don't know how they were able to dance. She was short and had a small frame and her hair was just right. It took her all day at the salon to get the latest hairstyle--cut bangs and a French roll. She recalls it was a big night. Billy Eckstein was in town and everybody in the beauty shop was going to the ballroom for some singing and dancing.

My father was standing in the back and the place had dim lighting. My mom and her girls walked into the ballroom slow and steady. They were feeling fine and looking good. She said she was just scanning the place. Ya' know how they do. Her girlfriend Gloria said, "Look at that guy! He is sharp!" He was getting ready to go onto the stage in about five minutes. As they were being seated at a table, their eyes met.

My mom said, "Oh yeah, he is cute!"

Her friend said, "I'm gonna meet him tonight." She said it out loud, as if she was marking her territory.

The table was right in front of the stage. As they were being seated, he saw them... I think my mom was stunned and tried to look away because her friend was very much interested, but he had eyes just for my mother. He was introduced as a local singer and he blew the house away with his deep smooth voice.

"*A Song for You*" was the next selection. He started to sing his songs of love and after the set was over, he began to walk towards the table, with his friend Milo (the owner of the club). My mom's friend Gloria whispered with her head turned straight, "He's coming over here, girl, he's coming!" Although she was very excited, he wasn't coming for her.

He wanted to meet my mom, and meet her he did! He asked Milo to introduce them, and he sat down at the table while all the other girls stared at the two of them talking. Then, one by one, they all got up to dance. You know how the Playa plays…and the band played on.

A love story was born that night and everyone there knew it. "Who's that girl with Snow?" as the natives of Newark called him. Someone would answer, "I think her name is Mary." They were inseparable after that night. She was accepted by his fragmented family, with all of their issues that laid dormant, waiting for the time to appear. And the protection of my father's brothers went for her as well. He asked her to marry him and that was a wedding to remember.

That union was made into a family and we were living what I thought was a normal and happy life…But shortly after that was when my uncle Maurice was killed and things really twisted. The changes were all becoming a ball of confusion.

What happened to my uncle Maurice proved to be tragic not only to him but to those he helped to shape…those younger siblings that often looked up to him for guidance. One night after gambling, he was shot and killed in cold blood. This event was a devastating thing for the family and nobody ever got over it.

After Maurice was killed, Brewster snapped. Trouble was adrenalin for him like alcohol was kryptonite for my father. When Otis's career was over and Maurice was no longer around, heroin became his neutralizer. My uncle Lloyd often tried to mimic Maurice so he separated himself from everyone else. As for my father, Maurice meant the world to him. He was responsible for my father getting into clubs where he did stand-ins and entertainment for stars at their private parties.

His dream was about to come true with a contract until the news of Maurice's death came. The business contract meant nothing to my father after Maurice was shot and my father was only hoping the killers would be found. Until the killers were caught, he just wanted to drop out of life.

My Aunt Margaret was now starting to display the affects of her mother's issues with men. Any issue my grandmother had with men was passed it on to Aunt Margaret. She influenced her in that way. My mom said she was beautiful when she was younger, her personality was very open, and her smile would light up a room. She no longer spoke of dreams and marriage, and children. She simply spoke when spoken to.

It was as if she did not exist any longer. It's hard to believe any one could have been so vibrant and alive and eventually lose a voice. Aunt Roberta also felt the loss and the loving care her older brother gave to his family but she proved to be the most resilient. She began to pour herself into her brother William whom she felt she had to protect.

By the time, my parents had two children and one on the way life was becoming a royal mess. My mother thought she saw a glimpse of a potential problem and tried to confront my father about it, early. He seemed to be still in control at that time, but he soon began to lose interest in singing, and that was just not normal for him, because he lived to sing.

Denial and self-deception about what was happening, under the surface added to the emotions and the issues of life he could not deal with. He had created a personality that was looking for a way out. This is where the self-deception was detected...He began to turn away from things he wasn't ready to accept. Slowly the self-destruction started to be his escape. How did this happen? He didn't have the ability to accurately judge simple situations. My mother was done with him...she had kids to think about.

I was too young to recognize my father's many faces of denial. He would put up a shield just to function. He didn't realize it was necessary to change anything. He hid where no one could get to him. Now as an alcohol and drug counselor, I understand the clinical definition of denial. It's a psychological defense mechanism in which confrontation with a personal problem or with reality is avoided by denying the existence of the problem or reality. His mother and sisters were his biggest enablers so he went to live with them.

I would visit my father from time to time when he was around and when we did have time together; it was memorable. Whenever I wanted to see him, it was always a big deal. I always had to get someone to pick me up because my mother wouldn't take me and no one else wanted to.

Early one Saturday morning my Aunt Roberta picked me up for the weekend and when we got to her house, my father was getting ready, because we were going out. I ran upstairs and he was shaving. I was banging on the door and he opened it with a million dollar smile. That's why they called him Snow because of his teeth. Now you would have to know my father to get this; every hair had to be in place and I do mean every hair even after a haircut. I should have known then he had issues with compulsive behaviors.

After gaining his undivided attention with a big hug, he looked down at me and I was all teeth (the two front ones were missing). Shaving cream was now all over my face.

"Daddy, look what you did!"

He laughed, my aunt laughed, and he said, "Let me finish Baby Girl, and we'll go to the park."

I sat on the steps and waited. He always called me Baby Girl, and I loved it. You know how kids are; don't tell them anything until your ready to deliver. Finally, he was finished shaving. Whew! It seemed like a long time.

"Are you ready yet?" I asked.

"Not yet," he said. My aunt called me downstairs and everybody started getting up to have a late breakfast. April, my favorite cousin was the first one at the table.

Aunt Margaret usually had little to say but everyone said she talked a lot when I came around. I always felt close to her because she made me feel special. We were getting ready for a late breakfast and I helped set up the table. My heart was beating louder than the noise from the forks and plates because I heard my father walking around upstairs and I could not concentrate on anything else. Then I heard his foot hit the steps and my Aunt Roberta said let him see you setting the table (this meant I was growing up and doing things).

I hesitated but I listened as he came around the corner into the kitchen and he just stared at me. I acted like I didn't see him. He said, "Come here, Baby Girl," and that was what I lived for. He kissed me, on the forehead, picked me up. He kept saying over and over again and everybody else joined in, "She looks just like Jessie" (my grandmother).

We went to the park right after brunch and he took me to his girlfriend's house. Now, you know I was going to tell my mother. He said she was his "friend." She was pretty. My father took me all over town that weekend to visit friends. He showed me where he was singing. One of the women he introduced me to really was a friend of the family. She was very nice to me and my dad said she was like one of his sisters. Her name was Edith McMurry. She said I could call her Miss Edy.

When my mom came to pick me up that Sunday, everyone from my dad's side of the family was there. My father came in with his "friend." I could see my mom was feeling a little uncomfortable. As for my dad, he hated for my mother to see him with someone. They both knew it was a waste of time. In her mind, he was calling for her, because he was in her heart, in her soul, and in her prayers. She thought it was something they had to go through in order to grow. She had made a decision and she was not going back…Even if her heart would skip a beat every time she saw him.

Soon after this weekend passed, our visits were few and far between. The battle with the alcohol was on and I could not compete. With this disease, there is no competition but just the embodiment of the desire. He was filled with the thought and desire to have it. Days, weeks, and months were going by and for about six months, I did not hear from him.

By this time, my mom was remarried and pregnant and my father definitely did not want to hear that. Anyway, as time went on my little sister Celeste was born. What was I suppose to do with that? She came around Christmas time and that was a bummer; we got pajamas for Christmas that year because money was tight mom said, and it all went to Celeste's crib, her diapers, and her bottles.

What kind of Christmas was that? I wanted to just pull my hair out. Being a family was very important to me and it kept the kids at school off my back. You know the question: Who's your daddy? I called my step dad by his first name, Ray. He worked well for appearances. I tried calling him dad, but my heart and my head were in two different places. He was nice and all but, I had issues -- gigantic ones.

At some point during this time, my father stopped returning my calls. (Of course, as a child I didn't know anything about alcohol being a disease. Now I know it is a dis-ease but a disease is a fact, it is not a truth. It is an experience but not a spiritual reality. That's what I know now. I knew nothing about "Relapse" back then and that it starts with isolation, shame, secrecy, resentment, insecurity, and fear. It all creeps in.

Communication is the key. If that starts to breakdown and there is no infrastructure to keep it all together, there will be a collapse. I began to worry when he hadn't returned my calls and the family was running out of excuses for him. I was starting to pester my aunt a lot. She assured me that she would make him get in touch with me and that was a long shot. She had to look for him because she really didn't know where he was. He had moved and didn't tell her where he was going. When she finally found him, he was living in a room with frostbite on two of his toes.

She immediately took him to the hospital where they amputated them. It was at that time that I was called. He was in the Veteran's Hospital in East Orange, New Jersey. I had heard about Jesus being a healer from my cousins and the Pentecostal church on the corner that had the tambourines and drums. I use to stand outside of the church just to hear the music and the clapping. I even stayed around to hear the women testify how Jesus healed their body, and how the devil tried to keep them down. My cousin Rhonda would say, "Get away from that door before you catch the devil."

We were all around seven years old. Fear was not present but I remembered hearing something about, Jesus the healer so I asked him to heal my father...And he did. After that, all I wanted to do is care for him...A little enabler in the making. At first, he didn't want me to see him, but I convinced him I could take it. He had a slight limp for a while, but as time went on it became a cool walk, again. I guess his alcoholism was dealt with while he was in the hospital.

Alcoholics Anonymous was introduced to him. He began to take on their twelve-step program and that's when we all started to notice a difference. He said he made a promise to God... I didn't even know he knew God! As a child, I didn't understand what it was all about.

These are the Twelve Steps from <u>Alcoholics Anonymous</u> that were introduced to my father.

    1. We admitted we were <u>powerless</u> over alcohol—that our lives had become unmanageable.

    2. Came to believe that a Power greater than ourselves could restore us to sanity.

    3. Made a decision to turn our will and our lives over to the care of <u>God</u> *as we understood Him.*

    4. Made a searching and fearless <u>moral inventory</u> of ourselves.

    5. Admitted to God, to ourselves, and to another human being the exact nature of our wrongs.

6. Were entirely ready to have God remove all these defects of <u>character</u>.

7. Humbly asked Him to remove our shortcomings.

8. Made a list of all persons we had harmed, and became willing to make <u>amends</u> to them all.

9. Made direct amends to such people wherever possible, except when to do so would injure them or others.

10. Continued to take personal inventory and when we were wrong promptly admitted it.

11. Sought through <u>prayer</u> and <u>meditation</u> to improve our conscious contact with God *as we understood Him*, praying only for knowledge of His Will for us and the power to carry that out.

12. Having had a <u>spiritual awakening</u> as the result of these steps, we tried to carry this message to alcoholics, and to practice these principles in all our affairs.

I didn't know about these steps back then but looking at these steps made me see that the most painful part of recovery maybe realizing how your abuse of a substance affects the people that you care about the most. Understanding what triggers affect a person is very important.

Chapter Three

THE NEED TO BE FREE

My father didn't realize that there was no need to be a prisoner of his feelings. If he wanted to find some rest, he would have to open up. Opening up is always the best way. Feelings of grief, anger, self-pity, shame, fear, guilt, and resentment were what he held inside. These things were being held inside and were not being released so they were slowly rotting him from the inside out.

He had so much of this locked up inside…His soul was on empty. He was shutting down and the mantra he gave himself was "the three D's: Don't talk, Don't trust and Don't feel." If he should talk, it would be the contents of his heart and those things were tucked away tightly.

If he should trust, he would be vulnerable and if he should feel, he would feel how he was falling short of his commitments. He was getting nearer to the bottom. My thought in the matter was like the Limbo, "How low can you go?" I heard it said like this: "Your soul can go so low you actually vacate the body."

The prodigal son in the Bible was unconscious. He had everything that most people long for, but it wasn't enough. How many people do you know like that? My father had not yet entered this state of mind. The bottom was still far way. My Aunt Roberta was no longer able to hold my father in one place. She had gotten married and my father decided to live with his brothers, Brewster and Otis.

One day Otis had a bright idea. Otis's friend, Tommy, came by one day and they all hopped in the car. Brewster and Tommy sat in the front and my dad and Otis were in the back. Tommy made a stop; Brewster went into the bank on Broad and

Market Street. Otis got out to buy a hotdog. He went in the bank to see what was taking Brewster so long.

Tommy was looking worried. Dad said, Brewster came up to the car walking fast and Otis had a stupid look on his face. They both jumped in yelling at the same time "Go Tommy!" My father said he just knew the cops were behind them but they weren't. He thought, "If they catch us, they're going to kill us." He said his heart was in his ears. He could hear it beating so loudly that he thought he had been shot already. They kept going…

It seems that it was all planned and my father had moved in at the wrong time. He said he was hungry and that's why he went with them. They were all supposed to be getting something to eat. It seems they even had a place to go to hide out and it was two weeks before they were apprehended. He never mentioned anything about the money at all. It was at that time my heart was longing for him and all of a sudden, he was no more…No calls and no contact whatsoever.

…As if, I didn't have enough to deal with: a new family, the incident at school with the name switch and then this happens.

My mother's friend Ruth called one Thursday night. I heard the phone when it rang and I was going to get it but my mom said she had it. It was her friend Ruth. Now Ruth and my mother grew up together and were more like sisters than friends.

"Mary, did you see the paper today?" "The front page of the Star Ledger?"

"No why?"

"Snow and his brothers are on it"

"What!"

"Yea girl, there was a robbery a couple of weeks ago and they were connected to it. Well, that's what the paper said."

"Not William!" My mother said "That's not him; he wouldn't do anything like that. It just doesn't make sense." All she could think of was, "What am I going to tell Toni?"

So she kept it a secret for about a year. My brother wondered, for a while but soon put it out of his mind because he had football activities that kept him very busy. After many attempts to contact my father with no avail, I was lost.

Chapter Four

GET A LIFE

Then one day, out of the blue the phone rings…

"Mom, telephone!" Gary yelled downstairs.

"Alright I'll get it!" she yelled back.

"Mary, this is Roberta. Mom died and I just wanted to tell you in case you wanted to bring the kids up. Everybody's going to be here and they would like to see the kids."

My mom said, "Roberta it's going to be tough, but for Jessie I'll do it."

Everybody called my grandmother Jessie--Miss Jessie, that is. I remember when my mom told me and Gary the news, Marsette was four at that time and somewhere sleeping. "Your grandma passed and we are going to the funeral...Do you want to go?" she asked hesitantly.

"Yes!" I said with excitement because I knew my father loved his mother and everybody goes to funerals. They would come from miles away and my father would be there. I could not wait to get dressed. I had a new dress, a pair of new shoes, and my hair was washed and pressed...real straight. Got burned on the ear a couple of times from the heat of the straightening comb 'cause I could not and would not keep still.

I was going to see my father. I was ready before anybody else was. I was thinking to myself, "What's taking them so long?" My brother was dressed up too, but he was moving slow on purpose. I wanted to pinch his arm but my mother would have loved to have an excuse not to take us. No way! I was going to be good.

"You all ready?" she asked looking at us again. I kept thinking to myself that I wish I could drive, because she drove so slowly. But I just smiled. We listened to the "behave yourselves" speech-- Don't talk about our home business, use your manners, and no yelling. When we arrived, it looked like a sea of people. I didn't know anybody at all. I was looking for my dad, William Holmes.

We got out of the car and my mothers eyes were on me. She knew my father would not be there, but I didn't. Still looking...Still looking...Still looking...But no Uncle Brewster. No Uncle Otis yelling to my mother, "Hey sister-in-law!" Then, I saw my Aunt Roberta. "Hey Mary," she said as she kissed her on the cheek. I was kind of upset with her because she could not find my father...In a year?

What did you do with him; he didn't just disappear? They all thought I was stupid. He must have been somewhere drinking and he had said that he'd stopped. Last time he lost two toes, what's it going to be this time a leg? As we were moving towards the family car, getting ready to go to the viewing, my aunt said let the kids ride with the other grandchildren.

My mom agreed, with hesitation, thinking I was going to say the wrong thing in the other car. I didn't, but I thought my aunt had a surprise for me when we got there. My brother got ready to say something smart but he looked at me and I was not smiling, I would have let him have it.

When we arrived, I saw it was a big place and everyone went in the front door but we went in the side door because I had to make a stop. My mother, my brother, and I started towards the front. Well, what we thought was the front. We went in a room and stood at the back of the parlor. There was no one in there, but four plain-clothes detectives and two cops, my father and his brothers.

They were brought in for the viewing of their mother, but they were supposed to be slipped out of the back door before everyone arrived. Somehow, I was able to get a glimpse of a man, which I later realized was my dad. Because we went into the wrong door, we were able to have what some would call a chance encounter.

I'll never forget it...The Funeral Director's office was down in the front where my father was standing. We walked into the funeral parlor from the back (my mother, my brother, Gary, and I). There they were...all three of Jessie's sons: William, Otis, and Brewster standing in the front with their backs turned to us.

I could hear some faint sobbing between the three sons...All at the same time as they looked at their mother lying in the casket, that they probably helped put her in. Four son's gone. Three in jail and one shot to death. How unbearable that must have been for her heart. Nevertheless, there stood Jessie's boys. That's who they were.

Their hands were cuffed in the middle of their backs and that was all that I could see. It might have been too much for a mother, as for the little girl longing to spend time with her daddy it definitely was because it broke my heart.

My father didn't see me but when the sound of someone sobbing towards the back of the room was heard, they all turned around (literally at the same time). It was me…The tears would not stop…The whole scene froze…It was like a moment in time that stood still…When he looked at me his eyes pierced something in my heart that made me know that nothing would ever make sense in my life unless he said something to me. Before they would take him out of the room, I just had to say something to him…before he went away…before it was too late and I could never find him again.

My father looked ashamed and embarrassed, not only because he couldn't hug me, but because everything was so wrong and twisted. It appeared that my grandmother was not the only dead person in the room. It was truly a scene where dead men were walking. I let go of my mother's hand and ran down front…I hugged him. I felt the cold cuffs and the officers trying to pull me away but they knew this had to happen…For me that was a divine appointment. The spirit was moving and no one could do anything about it.

The officers had allowed me and my brother to go in the back to see him and my father was able to hug us. Not knowing after that encounter, my life would forever be changed... My mother told me she wished she had never brought me to the funeral. Let me tell you, I was a little messed up later that afternoon. It was just all too much for me to process. The rest of the day, I was trying to sort out what actually happened.

At the repast, family members were coming up to my mom saying, "Girl you haven't changed a bit!" "Haven't seen you since I don't know when." "What have you been doing?" "You look great Mary." "Thanks," she said. "Just raising these kids."

It was so noisy in the kitchen. I just wanted to run as far away as I could. My mom told my uncle Lloyd to talk to me. Gary was with our cousins playing. My uncle Lloyd came into the kitchen. I saw him but I didn't feel like talking. He looked so much like my dad and he was so handsome. I remember thinking, "Why couldn't my dad be like him?" I really don't remember the conversation now, but evidently, I ignored my uncle because my mom said he didn't understand why I was so withdrawn. He said to my mother, "I know Jessie took care of her and all but how come she's so upset?"

Uncle Lloyd never saw the brothers at the funeral home because they were slipped out the back door. It was my uncle Lloyd who was able to get them out. He didn't want to see them. Looking around at the family there, I saw so much talent. I never knew my Uncle Lloyd's daughter, Marie, could sing like she did. She sang at the funeral and she blew the place away. I started to remember things as time went on that day. I remember looking at her while she was singing and thinking that the notes seemed to be coming from a deep place. Cousin Marie started to cry as she ended the selections because they were songs my grandmother loved.

Once we got back to the house, I was introduced to people from near and far. I knew I would never see them again, but I was polite. The doorbell was constantly ringing. Then my Aunt Roberta's friends started coming in with food. She was introducing them to everybody. She would introduce me by saying; "This is my favorite niece, Toni." She would then tell them her nephew Gary was somewhere playing. Her friends from high school remembered me from when I was a baby and from being over there on the weekends. They kept saying, "Hey, that's William's daughter, right?"

When I heard that, it snapped me out of it. "That's right, I belong to him. I am William's daughter," I said to myself.

"She looks just like her father." I loved that. My father may not have been there but he existed. If he were here, I would be standing right next to him.

My cousin, Marie, noticed I had been looking at her, so she walked over to me, and said, "Hey, little cousin."

"Hey," I said.

"Wanna go for a walk?"

"Ok," I said.

We went outside. It was a warm day, the sun was out, and I noticed there was a breeze blowing. Gary was playing kickball and if mom saw his clothes, he would be in big trouble. He wasn't important at that time, even if he was gonna get yelled at. My cousin and I kept walking and she began to tell me that my dad was her favorite uncle.

She said they'd always talked about doing a record together. She was sorry for all that had happened. She said, "Uncle William and I got the voice in the family, unless you can sing." I quickly said no. She laughed and said that my father always talked about all of us with her. Marie lived in Newark, right around the corner from my Aunt Roberta. She spent a lot of time with my father, sober and not so sober. She wanted me to feel close to him by talking about him. It did help. Somehow, the day started to change. I remembered my grandma Jessie…

It was getting late so we said our goodbyes and headed towards home. My mother was especially nice to me. Gary was his usual goofy self but even he left me alone (with a warning from my mom). Once we got home, my mother talked to me after we all got settled in and she had attended to Marsette and Celeste.

My parents knew that Marsette was too young to know anything of the world around her. Celeste, or Cee as we call her, was the baby then. Marsette was supposed to be the last baby but after my mother remarried, she said Celeste was the last.

It was a short conversation but she knew me well enough that whatever she said to me would relax me enough to go to sleep. Tomorrow is another day. It was after that day my mother decided to tell me the truth about where my father had been and why he went to jail. She needed time to adjust to the day herself. She had no idea that he was going to be there. My brother Gary even had some questions. My eyes were fixed on his face and I slowly drifted off to sleep.

The brightness of the sun woke me up. My mom was up early that day because it was Sunday. We were going to church with my Nana, which is my mother's mom. I wanted to go because Nana always promised that if we went with her we would stop by my Aunt Reesie's house in Newark after church. Aunt Reesie was my grandfather's sister.

Everybody wanted to go there because Aunt Reesie and Cousin Henrietta (Aunt Ressie's daughter) always cooked for us. Cousin Buddy was known for his cigars. Cousin Henrietta and her husband, Buddy, had four children that were all around our ages (Brian, Carol, Rhonda, and Irene). All of their kids looked just like the two of them. They always looked like little "Henry-Budds" running around.

When we got there, we had to wait a minute or two for everybody to get out of church. We sat on the porch knowing they would be coming around the corner at any minute. Aunt Reesie would be at the window smiling in her rocking chair. I knew what was waiting in the kitchen but we had to wait for the Aunts…And then they appeared as they bustled around the corner.

"Here they come!" we'd yell. Peggy, Barbara, Cynthia and my Auntie Della…They were "sanctified." They wore the doilies, the long dresses, and those light stockings. Nobody's legs were that color. They had their tambourines in their hands and big smiles on their faces. We were Baptist they were Holiness. I was seven. Sounds like the Hatfield's and the McCoy's or something. I noticed they were all "big boned" And boy they could eat. Everyone came over there after church because that was the place to be.

My Cousin Tommy came over too (Aunt Reesie was his mother). He and his wife, Tweedy had four boys (Daryl, Tommy, Tyrone, and Durant). Sounds like Happy, Sleepy, Dopey, and Bashful (that would be Daryl). When we all got together, it was fun and food galore but this Sunday was a little different. I was listening to my cousins laugh and talk about things they were doing, but my mind kept drifting to thoughts of my father and when I would see him again.

In church, I had asked Jesus to protect him and to let him know that I missed him. I started to think about writing him so, I decided when I got home I would ask my mother about it. During all this thinking, I found a ray of hope. I was ready to go.

"Come on Nana can we go?" I asked. An hour after that we were on our way.

Finally, we were in front of our house, "Bye Nana!"

"Tell your mother I'll call her later!" She yelled.

My grandmother dropped us off because she didn't like to drive in the dark so she was hurrying home. As we were walking in the door, I saw Marsette crying. Her tears were always huge. This time she was eating ashes from the ashtray. My mother and Ray smoked and my mom took the ashtray from her. Now she was having a fit. She was always doing that. Celeste was on a blanket on the floor.

The house was filled with the scent of Sunday dinner. There was a choice of smoked turkey in collards and candied yams, potato salad, fried chicken and barbecued chicken. Gary was greedy and always wanted the leg, which was his favorite part of the chicken. Jiffy cornbread…My mom cooked it especially for Gary and me. We liked to eat and that was one of our favorite meals. Mom was really setting me up for one of our one to one talks later on that night. Gary as usual made a mess by dropping the lemonade. I wasn't laughing too hard because I just didn't feel like it.

We were talking about church and some lady passing out and how I got scared when another lady yelled, "Amen, Praise the Lord!" I asked, "Why do they sing those slave songs during communion?" That's what my Grandmother said they were. The one I remember most is *"A Charge to Keep I Have and a God to Glorify."* She said there was a time when there was no music and people had only their voices. Their lyrics were signals to the slaves in the fields. We talked about seeing the cousins after church and mom asked how everybody was doing. We replied, "Good. They all said to tell your mother Hi!"

Dinner was over and we had to clean up after ourselves. Gary acted like he was going to tell me to wash the dishes, but it was his turn. See what I mean, always trying to start something. He wanted to play as usual.

"Let's talk," mom said as everything was done in the kitchen.

"Alright" I said as we went upstairs to my room.

"Let's talk about yesterday alright?"

She began to speak about choices and how everything came about and not knowing when and where everything went wrong. I waited for her to finish and asked the magical question. She was being so soft and sweet, I thought she was going to give me whatever I asked for.

"Can I go see him?"

"No!"

Then I asked, "Can I write him?"

She hesitated then she said, "I'll look into it."

I think I was satisfied with that answer. I don't think a "No" would have been a good idea at that time, especially knowing the 15 years my father was facing. He had never been to jail before this incident. It had affected me deeply and my mother saw that. She worked with me.

Monday came around and it was time to go to school. As usual, Gary was running late because he never wanted to go to bed at night and he never wanted to get up the next morning. He walked me to school and told me not to worry about dad because he could take care of himself. He tried to assure me that he'd be coming home soon. I asked, "How do you know?"

He said mommy had talked to him and so did Uncle Lloyd. Mommy and Uncle Lloyd said it would best if we don't go see dad. "Maybe you can write him," he said. I just looked at him, because after that he said he didn't want to write. We were silent the rest of the way. I was trying not to think about my mother making the necessary calls so that I could start writing.

The day was not ending fast enough but I knew that sooner or later it had to end. After gym class, it was almost time to go home. "Come on 2:30. Alright 2:30 bell." I said to myself. My heart was beating fast. "Gotta get downstairs 'cause Gary's picking me up. Can't be late." But when I got down stairs, Gary wasn't there. I just knew he was off somewhere playing. I found him by the side of the school playing some stupid tag. "Come on let's go!" I yelled.

He was walking regular and I was walking fast trying to keep up. He asked me why I was rushing, 'cause we weren't going anywhere? I told him that I wanted to see if I could write a letter that night. He looked at me and said, "You're stupid. Race you!" We started running. Of course, he won. Mom was home. Whew!

I was happy to see her. She had good news for me and that night I would write my first letter. There were rules and the Warden had given my mother guidelines. I was excited and my mom had gotten me some paper and a pencil. I started writing within 10 minutes. It was an "at last" feeling and the excitement was coming back. "Dear Daddy…" I think I wrote four pages before I was satisfied. I got a stamp and an envelope and that night Gary and I walked to the corner mailbox. I pulled the lever back and dropped it in myself.

It had been more than a week with no response but on the ninth day there was mail for me. It had tape on the back as if it was opened. I just glanced at that. I ripped it open and started to read it. It started with these lines "To my dear baby girl"…We started from there and the letters were so filled with what I needed.

Some things he explained I understood. Some things I didn't understand. Like not having to worry about where he was or what he was doing. I began to see things differently. His questions over time became funny because things were changing, and things were not like they were when he first went in. Everything must change. I was able to deal with school and I also kept my last name. Activities at school became fun because I had something else to talk about.

Even if everyone turned their back on my father, I was not going to. For the next 13 years, my father and I caught up as we continued our correspondences.

Chapter Five

WHO WILL ROLL AWAY THE STONE

My mother said I was never at a lost for words. I have always had an opinion about things. It's just that as a child you're told you should be seen and not heard. The circumstances for me were quite different. You see I had a captive audience. As the years passed by, I actually got to know a lot about my father. He was able to "come out of hiding" so to speak. His senses were making a connection. I was not aware of the process of change or better yet the hand of God orchestrating the change. Finally, I could see some of what had occurred in him.

All of that now makes more sense. Perhaps back at the age of seven, I was in a world of "Imagination and No Tomorrow," and it was quite a hopeless state. I guess this is where my father had to out grow his fixed ideas. It's only after you awaken that you will start to remember.

As I noticed in my father's letters, he had begun to recall things. Some things he liked and some he didn't like. He talked about things he didn't have a chance to experience. The numbness was starting to wear off like anesthesia. Feelings started to come back and wow, he was aware. As I saw these changes, I just worked with it.

Things on the outside are changing fast, my father would say. I just let him tell me what he was feeling. Talking with me was a relief for him. He was able to be himself and I let him find his way…The light was there. "When you awake you start to remember."

By the age of thirteen, I was in junior high school trying to find my identity. My friends and I decided to put together a singing group. I don't remember the name of the group. Anyway, I wrote my father about it. He thought it was a good idea and he gave me some pointers. I could tell he didn't like talking about singing--he'd sort of skim over the subject most of the time so, I didn't push it at that time. I was never more excited when we got booked for the talent show after one of our auditions. Sherry, Dawn, Denise and Terry, ran home to tell their parents and I went home to tell mine.

It seems like my letter got to my father faster than normal. The response I got was also fast. He said good things about our ideas. He knew all about stage fright so he told me things about being calm. He said the bigger the star the more nervous he was. Billy Eckstein made him the most nervous even though Mr. Eckstein said to him one night, "You sound like me." Count Basie said he was singing his notes. My mom used to tell me that about him too. This was all I talked about until the event was over.

My brother came to the show and he sat in the back. He said he only came so I would not have to walk home by myself. When the performance was over, I asked him, "How did we do?" He said that we were all right. I just punched him in the shoulder and we laughed all the way home. We had plenty to talk about because of the other singers that should have gotten the curtain that night.

At times, I could feel a detachment from my father. I now know it was depression, which is common in recovery. I read that U.S prisons are overflowing, at least in part, due to the number of substance abuse individuals who are confined there. I also read, while researching, that studies have indicated that the highest proportion of high risk situations for alcoholics involve interpersonal negative emotional states, while the highest proportion of high risk situations reported by heroin addicts involve social pressure (Marlette and Gordon- 1985).

My father had to find a way not to remember the former things; nor consider the things of old. His children were all growing up and he could not be apart of the experience. I don't remember ever hearing about Al-Anon Family meetings growing up. I see how it could have been helpful.

The older I got I started thinking about the people who were incarcerated with my father. I wondered if they had children. What were they going through? He said he stayed pretty much to himself and that some of the men he associated with did have children but they hadn't seen or heard from them in years. That really bothered me because I was feeling for them.

"Dad, can't you just talk to them about their kids? You can tell the guys to write or call their kids but don't just give up. Tell them to do something or try something, at least to let their kids will know that they did try? Let the kids see it, put it in their minds?"

My father said, "Whoa all of their circumstances are different, honey."

He understood how I was feeling and said he would try talking to them and we would talk about it later and for me not to worry about that.

As the years kept moving by, I didn't realized why I had been so concerned. I had no idea I was preparing for prison ministry. I always thought about my father during holidays. I'd often wonder, "What are they feeding him today? "Is he sad like me?" It was the Wednesday before Thanksgiving. I went to get the mail and there was something waiting for me. It was a card my dad had made. One of the prisoners was an artist. The card was beautiful. You could tell he put a lot into it, because of the details. It said, "For my kids during Thanksgiving, Love you much."

It took him so long to do this, to get up the courage but that's part of the 12 steps to get back into the game of life. Believing all things are possible. I was about 15 then and I was at the "When can I date stage?" From a jail cell, I heard "no dating, just be still and know." My dad was not having that and my mom said that at 16, life is just starting to get interesting. My father didn't say much about me dating anymore. As for me, I was only asking.

Countdown…Three more years to go. I saw the years as they went by and the time we tried to capture. A lot happened during those years. I was now 18 and as Maya Angelou would say, "Life ain't been no crystal stairs." I got pregnant then at 21 and entered into a marriage that did not last. My father assured me everything would be all right. He said an abortion would be out of the question. It is what it is. My father was getting prepared to come home and in recovery sometimes, a person's environment is the most important thing.

How is this supposed to work? Panic was trying to set in. How is he going to adjust? Where is he going? He assured me he would not drink again. I didn't know then what I know now. It's said that as much as 54% can be expected to relapse in AA or NA, 61% will have multiple relapse, and 12% will relapse within the first year. Relapse is referred to as returning to the pattern.

My brother had gone to visit our father from time to time. He was a man now and he did what he wanted to do. Time was winding up. Getting out was getting close and there was tension in the air. My father was getting scared with all of the thoughts, the pressure, and the expectations. I was twenty then and he felt I didn't need him any more. A year to go and I was getting anxious. Maybe a little scared, I don't remember that exactly.

Who knew what the feelings were that floated around? All I knew was if there were going to be any expectations then God would have to place them. The ingredients my father needed I did not have. I'd begun my spiritual journey for that which was greater than anything I had ever known. It had nothing to do with whether something magical happened and was not concerning my father. I just knew something was missing from my life, and when I made that connection there was nothing to be desired. I was spiritually awakened.

I was not looking for a church home; I was looking for the owner of the building. The spirit of the living God! And when He found me, I was no longer fragmented. This was what I knew my father needed. So I talked to him about how my life had changed, he listened.

Life is funny. You can move through it with your eyes shut if you want to. That's called being an on-looker not a participator. That's when you let people define you and tell you what you are because you have no idea. When you awake, you will remember.

"What will I remember?" I hear you saying. You will remember you were on assignment and you had a purpose. Jesus came remembering who he was and that's why the people of that day were so angry with him. Jesus said that he and the Father were one and that he came to seek and save that which was lost. He also said that, "They that are whole need not a physician." We, on the other hand, came forgetting--wandering around in the dark and not knowing who we are.

The prison system reminds us of the dry bones. The veil, the man of Gadara out of his mind, Lazarus a dead man walking, Nicodemus an undercover believer, Jonah the runaway, Rahab the prostitute, Moses the killer, Lot's wife wanting to hold on to the past. Then there was Peter's denial, Judas the backstabber, David and Bathsheba creepin' in the night, Jacob the liar, Sampson and Delilah's passions, Solomon and all his wives, Jezebel the seducer, the Roman soldiers don't know why they did what they did, and the Devil surely you know his M.O.

What do you really think the cross represents? When you look at them, you want to ask, "Where is God?" When *they* look at you *they* also ask, where is God? They look at us and we are looking at them. What are we looking at? Everybody is looking for the living God who is moving over the face of the waters and brooding through the land. Just because we can't see Him in each other doesn't mean He's not within each of us. He is "I AM." Our job is to "Keep looking until He is uncovered in every man we see."

When my father was released, I looked at him, for the first time in 13 years, I saw God somewhere but he had to be awakened, and revealed. There are many things that can break a man's spirit. Call them excuses but anyone can arise. My father had life but it was not expressed." A lack of expression is depression" (The Laws of Thinking). Who do you know like that? They're living but you can't see any signs of life. The scripture says: "I Am Alpha and Omega." To me that represents something complete. In and out. To me that means God can complete the job He has started.

There are over three million people in prison, and some will eventually be released. Their connection to society is very important. Getting a job, health care, education, housing, and counseling, is critical. My father had some support but not everyone has that. "The Reminder," (society), is always there lurking. No matter how many years you spend out of prison society never allows you to forget. My father heard about Christ and accepted Him into his life then began to walk in it.

...Awake thou that sleepest, and arise from the dead, and Christ shall give thee light.

(Ephesians: 5:14)

I was determined to see my father whole. I am serving a living God. He is not away, He is not asleep. His Spirit is with us and within us.

In Him I am living and moving and have my being... There was no way I should expect anything less than what was being offered by the Spirit. Wholeness is in spirit, soul, and body. Resurrection in the fullest. I was building my faith as well as talking to my father often. Actually, it was necessary for him to reach out. He was now finally working. He felt better about that and so did I.

I really wanted to be near him especially after all that time. He started coming over on Fridays and going to church with me on Sundays. It was our time of bonding. This was really discipleship. I began to see signs of transformation. I finally started to see my father walk out a scripture that says:

Let this mind be in you which was also in Christ Jesus

(Philippians 2:5)

He was determined to believe that God was life to him and he had to firm up some things and rid himself of anything and everyone that contradicted that. Before he could enter peace, he had to walk out of his state of confusion. Which is to let go of people and events that get caught up in the web of your mind. He had to know that The Spirit in him was God. In order for God to lead the way, he had to reach for the grapes on the vine because they are higher and sweeter than the onions on the ground. He had to look up.

My father was learning how to manage his emotions. When a person is uneasy it may be because they feel they are being judged for everything, especially if they have burned a lot of bridges. Family is the last to let you go and most often than not that, bridge is the last to cross. The first step is to start where you are and go on from there. You then let the word of God set things in motion. I believe I saw some of those emotions surface as I watched my father's journey. I learned that "The soul must ascend to knowledge" (Bishop E Bernard Jordan).

I began to inquire of the Lord to teach me something about the *soul*. This was when my journey began. I was thirsty for the living water. I had heard of the soul being the seat of your emotions. I had heard that the soul was the seat of will and purpose. I have been taught that I am a spirit with a soul and I live in a body. I needed to grasp a full understanding of the soul. As I began to search, a few explanations began to surface.

It was definitely not this definition. Soul: instinctive quality felt by black persons as an attribute or inner music or soul brother or soul food (etymology dictionary). So, we see how context is very important here. There is no way after your soul is transformed that one should have an insatiable appetite for fried chicken, pig feet or collard greens or watermelon. That is definitely the wrong context...

I've learned "you can only have what you understand" because "you cannot go beyond your understanding." Change takes place because growth will demand it. The spirit is the high element and the soul is the lower element. The body is animated by the spirit and the soul (Vines dictionary). The spirit is the breath and the soul is the "stuff / substance." Let's look at this example: This concept helps to explain a state of transition. Take a quantity of water and freeze it into ice.

The Substance theory maintains that there is a substance, which is unchanged through this transition, which is in both the liquid water and also the frozen ice. It maintains that the water is not replaced by the ice-it is the same "stuff" or substance. If this is true, then it must be the case that the wetness of water or the hardness of ice is not essential to the underlining substance. Essentially, matter does not disappear; it only changes form (This Western Philosophical concept is based on a theory in basic Chemistry). The soul is transformed by the renewing of the mind.

My father also seemed to walk in a type of darkness of the soul. This could be a place where one is unfamiliar. Thus, you have "The Spirit Realm." This darkness has a few descriptions. One description I found was that contemplation means *"Interior Life."* There must be a focus to have the vision of God. So we must go within where it is dark.

...when thou prayest, enter into thy closet, and when thou hast shut thy door, pray to thy Father which is in secret; and thy Father which seeth in secret shall reward thee openly.

(Mathew 6:6)

This tells me what God is doing in me is none of your business. It's "our secret." I am getting my mind back. The closet is where the soul is in contemplation. The soul must be willing to let the reconciliation of the heart and mind becomes one true nature. There in lies the marriage. Sounds familiar? You cannot tell me who you are until you go within and God reveals it to you. Remember you've been asleep.

I needed to understand for myself that my father was sleepwalking. Truth be told, I too was asleep and was awakened but we must all rise individually. So, I inquired of the Lord and I found this:

I remembered reading a scripture about my soul making her boast in the Lord when it is cast down within me. What did that mean for me? So I inquired of the Lord and this is what I found: Your skull is the tomb where Christ is asleep that's why we must renew our mind. Only then will you truly know who you are. One day you will know the Mystery of the resurrection when you rise within yourself. For the only grave Christ is buried is in your own skull. That's why we are to have the mind of Christ

This journey or discovery is my experience as I watched my father transform. Little by little, he started reaching for what was rightfully his. He was an heir to salvation. That can sound a little crazy when you're making $5.00 an hour, but the objective here would be to know who you are and walk in that light. Sounds like a step in the dark, doesn't it? But it is yet another purification process, another dark place where you develop night vision.

I have been taught that this place is called "uncreated light" (Catholic Encyclopedia). Only here, knowledge of God is offered unto man. It is here where your five senses are not needed. The mysteries of God are hidden in the darkness. Your eyes are reshaped to adapt, thus, the eye of your understanding will be opened.

I've found that the soul can be stirred by an inkling of God's presence even though the mind sits in darkness and does not understand anything. This is "dark purification." Love only God can give and your soul takes it all in. The soul can tell it is seriously wounded, by a powerful love, but it cannot grasp it.

My father was experiencing some seasons of imbalance. As I watched that, I inquired of the Lord and this is how I understood it: God himself walks with the weaker souls, now appearing and disappearing. Exercising them in his love. Without the turnings away, they would never learn to reach for him (Marabai Starr). When I think of the Soul on Empty, I think of one who operates in the senses only. A person who does not allow the soul to make her boast in the Lord.

In order to get the wisdom of the Spirit you have to be made ready for it. My father was being made ready. We all are being made ready. For the soul must be measured to see how much it can handle. I learned there is a part of us that is never fooled. I was reading one day and came across this poem. I'd never seen it before but I knew it.

When the house of sense was stilled, when through this blessed night of purification her passions were quenched when her desires had been laid to rest and fallen asleep, the soul could slip away at last and begin her journey along the spiritual path...(Marabai Starr)

My father started to spend more time with me on the weekends now because his appetite for the former things was changing. I really didn't get involved with the process; I was just there. I was actually working through my own life, to tell the truth. He was doing the reaching and life was calling. My father began to look at possibilities. You know, the "what ifs."

So, I inquired of the Lord, what next? Where do we go from here? This is how I understood it: Act as thou I AM and I will be. I have been taught that: poverty is a man without a dream (Bishop Jordan). So, we began to set goals such as getting another job and different living arrangements. He had gotten his own place and it was what he wanted to do.

My mom by this time had been divorced for a few years and she was quite happy. "So don't even look at me," she would say. My father on the other hand was getting his mind back and as the kids these days would say, "He got his swagger back." The change on the inside had begun to show up on the outside. What is done in the dark will be seen in the light. This was a good thing.

Everybody was going to be at my Nana's house on Sunday. There would be at least, a good 30 family and friends there that were all really coming to see my dad. So my mom asked me if he was coming. When I talked to him on Thursday, I asked him if he would go to Nana's house on Sunday he said yes.

"Look Toni," my father said anxiously, "Who's going to be there?"

"I don't know, Dad, but you've got to look sharp, real sharp"

"What's the matter, you don't like my clothes?"

"Yes, but you need more color." So my son, Troi, suggested we go to the mall.

During that time my little sister Marsette was all grown up now, married with two boys, Corey and Steven, and her appetite had changed drastically. No more cravings for ashes. Gary was living in New York and had a daughter named Tonyelle. Celeste was married with two children. Their names are Jared and Brooke. My son, Troi, and I were doing well.

I think my sisters' husbands were mentors to Troi in many ways. I gave them both a hard time when they had their eyes on my sisters but that was because we only had each other. Steve, Marsette's husband, was jogging one day when we saw him and I told her, "That's your husband."

She said, "You're crazy."

I said, "Stop the car."

I asked him his name and introduced him to my sister and BAM! Now they're married with children. Celeste's husband, Obbey, was her Mr. Tee. Remember him? They looked like Brutus and Olive Oyl when they got together (19 years and going strong). So our family structure was in place. The foundation was that of the Lord.

We finally convinced my dad to go to the mall. Saturday morning. He wanted to go and come back. You know I should have known Troi wanted to go to the mall for something. He got shoes, sneakers, a suit, a jacket, three pairs of pants, and a pair of jeans.

It was September and not cold yet, but school was starting and he was hitting his grandfather up for some cash. My father would take time out with his grandkids and spend money I knew he didn't have. I was shopping on my own. I saw a ring as my father was walking towards me and I noticed it because it was my name in diamonds.

"Wow!"

He quickly said, "Do you like that?"

"Yes!" I said.

"Try it on," he said. So I did.

"She'll take it." He told the clerk. I was speechless. Just like that. I was in a whirlwind of words and emotions.

"Here is your receipt sir." He took it.

"Thank you," he said and we left to go home.

I couldn't help but wonder where he got so much money? He was spending money all day but I squashed any doubt because I really did not know what to think. Troi talked the whole way about his stuff because he was grateful. I kept looking at this diamond ring on my finger, wondering... When I looked at my dad, he had this look on his face like, "Finally no limits."

Marsette was so sorry she didn't meet us at the mall. She didn't get anything so he gave her some cash. The grandsons all got cash. I still didn't say anything. Suddenly, it was Christmas in September at our house. We stopped and got something to eat on the way home and Marsette and the boys came over. Celeste and Obbey came with their crew. My brother Gary even showed up.

Of course no one at anytime knew when he was going to appear. We had a good time. I looked at my father's face and he was aglow. He was in a special moment in time. A moment he had really carved out for himself somewhere in his secret soul, waiting for the right time.

The doorbell rang and it was Mommy. Hey! Now this looks like a set up, Jesus style. So I inquired of the Lord, "What is this?" This is how I understood it years later: What you desire is already waiting for you, wrapped in silence and unseen (Bishop Jordan). We were laughing and catching up on stories, events, and things my father only read in our letters.

The doorbell rang again it and it was Steve. "Hey what's up man?" Hand shaken, hugs, and love were in the air .I looked at my dad and I heard in my heart: The only way a man can evolve is to let him alone and allow him to awaken to himself. Jesus said, "Behold I stand at the door and knock."

Chapter Six

IN MY MIND

The service that Sunday was really good. Everybody was in the hallway and the vestibule of the church trying to get a tape of the message. I don't know how we got up on time, since we all went to bed so late. For some reason, my father was excited and ready to go. He got us all up. Gary had spent the night and went to church with us because of the big dinner Nana was having, but that wasn't until 3:30pm. We went home to change clothes then we ate breakfast and sat around.

Gary was outside cleaning out his trunk and talking on the phone with his daughter, Tonyelle. He was telling her how much he loved her and would see her later at Nana's house. I looked at my father thinking how I could strike up a conversation about mom.

I started with, *"Dad, did I see a spark last night?"*

"What? He said real fast.

"Okay, if you don't want to tell me, then that's ok." I said it, but I didn't mean it.

"Listen, I was just conversing with your mother. Besides, you know your mother."

"He has something going on in his mind," I said to myself. He understood that sometimes you must let things marinate.

"What time is it?" He asked.

"It's about 3 o'clock," I said.

"Are you almost ready?" he said calmly.

"Yes," I answered as I was scrambling around. I ran upstairs to get my wallet.

"Okay," he yelled back, "I'll put the dishes in the dishwasher."

"Okay, thanks." I came downstairs and we left.

My grandmother's house was about 10 minutes away. Gary drove his Mercedes. It was his pride and joy; it was a classic. He had it completely remodeled. His car was beautiful. It was cream with cream interior and it had chrome everywhere. Anyway, we road in his car. We got to the house and people were pulling up from everywhere. This reminded me of the prodigal son. "Somebody go kill the fatted calf," I was thinking as we were walking up the driveway. We could smell the barbeque and that meant somebody had fired up the grill in September.

There were still some flowers in bloom. I was kind of surprised, but then again at my grandmother's house there are flowers blooming throughout the year. We walked inside. "Hey Mom, hi Nana", I said. Everybody was hugging and glad to see my dad. I had my left eye on my mother because neither she nor my father said anything to any of us as to whether or not anything was going on. I was beginning to be suspicious. They made their way to each other through the crowd. We all knew something was mixing.

Gary walked in after we did. "Hey everybody!" He had been outside looking at his car. I wanted to smack him. He wanted to move the car because the kids wanted to play. I said, "Gary, go move the car so you can relax." He then turned around and said, "You think so?"

My mom went into my grandmother's room to get some pictures. As she was coming out of the room with a stack of pictures, we knew this time we were gonna really bust up laughing because we all had changed so much. It's always funny because pictures don't lie. We were looking at pictures of ourselves as we remembered the past. My father was looking at pictures of his life for the first time since his thinking had begun to change. It made a difference in his surroundings.

I realized what you decide to meditate on day and night is your business but it's been my experience that old thoughts produce the same old habits. It becomes obvious to everyone around you if you did not change your mind. I had read that it takes 30 days to break a habit. About a year had passed, and my father was at the stage in his life where he was beginning live in the present. I saw a new determination coming out of him.

He grabbed hold of what God was pushing towards him. I was not yet sure of what the determination was for, but he was persistent and specific in looking towards my mother. All of a sudden, the reach looked shorter for him and possible. Focus was working for him and he was going to use it until he could prove it. He was looking for that place where he could say with all of his heart, "I know in whom I believe." At some point, we must know that we know. My father now desired a better life.

My sister Celeste came in the door with her family and yelled, "Didn't I just see you all last night?" Wait, in walks four more (Rhonda, my cousin with her husband, Sharik, and my cousin Daryl with his wife Sandy). It got crazy in there. All of the pictures were being passed around and we were laughing at each other. My mother was giving out warnings to everybody not to pocket her pictures. There were wedding pictures mixed up in there and my father got a hold of a few. I must admit, it was strange seeing him take a step back.

I really didn't know just how much of a trigger this whole scene would be. I have grown to know every step must be tried. With every step, there is a turning, a turning away from the old and an embracing of the new, even if you have no idea of what the new holds for you.

There was no reason for my father to be afraid to look at his past. His mind was made up. Fear of anything had vanished. This was remarkable because at what point does the thirteenth step kick in. Here it was right in front of me. Glancing at the past is just a measurement of how far you've grown. The food was smelling good and we all had to break up the party to help set up the tables outside.

My father was talking to family members who knew him when he was singing. Some knew he had been in jail and some did not. They just thought my parents broke up. Everyone was having a good time and I was excited about the whole day. I was actually embracing a moment in time that somewhere in my secret soul I knew was supposed to be. Recovery involves everyone.

The person in recovery is the only one who decides when they are ready to let others in. My father was ready for this party. I always heard it put like this: "When the student is ready the teacher appears." (Author Unknown) I guess this is true for all things. I read where a philosopher of old had written: "All things be ready if the mind is so."

My father was getting his consciousness ready for more, but there is always *"The Reminder."* You know someone ready and willing to stir up your past. My father was talking to someone named Teddy, a relative had brought from Newark, and he remembered him. This is how the conversation went:

Teddy said with excitement, "Yeah you know Newark is not the same anymore. Things sure changed fast. Do you remember the club on Belmont Ave in Newark? Man, that place use to be jumping. I was there when Joe Williams used to stop in frequently. They don't have places like that any more." My father didn't contribute to that too much not really wanting to get into the nostalgia. *Yet this is just another test*

But Teddy insisted," I'm still trying to find out where I know you from."

My dad said, "I used to sing there."

"Yeah, that's where I seen you. Didn't you get caught up in something with your brothers or something? This was years ago I'm talking about?"

My father said, "That was me."

"Did it all have something to do with a bank?"

My father said, "Yeah."

"Hold up," Teddy said, "They never did recover that money."

My father said, "Really?"

Teddy looked at my father and said, "You slick dog. Where are your brothers?" Teddy kept on prying.

"Well" my father explained, "Brewster and Otis were released 10 months ago and within that time Brewster fell and hit his head on the sidewalk and died. Otis was shot on the corner of Broad and Market Street in Newark by two cops in broad daylight."

My father was learning to deal with things by talking them out and this was just the beginning…

Chapter Seven

PASSION FOR A NEW POSSIBILITY

My father had begun to make mental moves towards New Brunswick, New Jersey where I lived. Newark was not really a place he desired to be any longer. He had outgrown his surroundings and he was ready to make the physical move. My father and mother had been talking with really no encouragement from my brother, my sister, or myself. Only because this was something my mother said she was not interested in, so we didn't expect it. Twenty-one years had gone by and who would have ever thought there could be a slight chance. No one saw this coming. I guess, as Ernest Holmes says, "The only limits are the ones we acknowledge."

My father began to reach and he didn't think for one minute he couldn't have whatever he was reaching for. This was certainly a new man. I'd never seen such determination or a will to do.

I could tell he was making his way towards New Brunswick when he said to me "I'm going to look for a place out here."

"Oh, okay," I said, "have a place in mind Dad?"

"Nope," he said, "just going to look."

One day, I think it was on a Monday; my father called and said he was coming on a Thursday instead of Friday. He was going to meet with my mother. Now this was a little strange because they were not really open about anything. Things were getting a little obvious, my mother and father were purposely sitting together at church. She started inviting him for dinner on Sundays after church.

You see my father had been home two and a half years, and my mom and he stayed clear of each other. Or so it seemed. She was at a distance in space but the heart was never that far.

So as time went on, no one else began to matter because he was being tried by her standards. Boldness, poise, and confidence on his part began to show and in the midst of all that, somewhere down deep he would say to himself, "You don't deserve this." He would have to resist that and say, "I've changed, I'm not the same."

One day he announced, "I want to learn how to drive!" Just like that. We were all stunned…Drive? Gary had come by with his daughter, Tonyelle. My Aunt Royelle had stopped by with her daughter, Dee Dee. It was a Friday and I had fried fish. My mom was at the salon late that night and my father wanted to go pick her up. He knew doggone well that he could not drive. We were saying to him jokingly take some driving lessons so we don't have to go through all of this. We thought it was funny but he didn't. So all of a sudden, he said, "Tomorrow let's look into it." So I said, "Okay, Dad."

It was quite chilly outside. It was my father's birthday but he did not allow me to make a big deal about it. Somehow, I knew this one was special. It happened to fall on a Saturday this year. My father had mentioned that he wanted to take driving lessons but we never gave it much thought. Who's going to teach him? Troi was sixteen by this time so he couldn't. That means it was left up to Marsette, Gary, or myself. Gary would not let him wreck, I mean practice with his car. That was not going to happen.

Gary was sweating and in the corner of the living room. He said to me, "Don't even try it Toni." We could not escape this new man. He was fierce and was not taking no for an answer. So we, meaning Gary, Marsette, Celeste, and I paid for driving lessons. He thought that was so nice and thoughtful. We knew in our hearts that it was purely selfish. That was his birthday present.

This was getting crazy. He started taking lessons every Friday and Saturday as soon as he would arrive at our house. He took lessons for two months. No one wanted to ask him how he was doing. And he would not tell us either. The frustration was obvious. It took him a long time. I'm really not sure how long, but he took the written test two times. Troi was the only one who could tolerate him during this frustrating time because Troi was also taking the test.

My father did not want my mother to know that he was even thinking about taking driving lessons. The difference with the frustration was that he was working it out through acknowledging it and anyway he could without drinking or retreating into himself.

"Wow, when this is over," he said. I'm getting a car.

"Oh Lord!" I said to myself, "I've got to call Gary." When I called him he said, "When he gets his license he will not be coming over for awhile." Just like Gary to say something like that.

The day came for him to take the driving test. My father came by early Friday, January 30th. My mother's birthday was that very weekend. Oh please, none of us saw this coming. This was an important day. Is he or isn't he getting his license? Gary called and said he had something to do so he couldn't take him. Marsette was working and Celeste was out with Obbey, her husband. I was home waiting. This is where he's been every weekend for three years. Marsette's husband, Steve, took dad for the driving test. There was a knock at the door and it was them. My father finally passed the test and he got his license!

Eventually, we went to sleep that night. It was a milestone in my father's life. This was big; this was huge. He did something he never thought he would do. He could not wait to tell everybody, and I do mean everybody. Then, mom's birthday had arrived. It was freezing cold outside but there was no snow. Gary called early.

"Mom's birthday is today, are you coming to Jersey?" I asked.

"Uh," he started stuttering.

"Snap out of it," I said laughing. "He will not ask you if he could drive your car, he's already volunteered me."

Gary was yelling, "I told you! I'll be there at 4...Later," he said laughing as he was hanging up the phone.

My father was up at the crack of dawn. I don't know why, excited maybe. He had shaved and dressed by 6:00 am...What the heck? This man is crazy! I was happy for him and all but, what is he going to do next? I couldn't stop thinking about my car. I'd had it for only six months (a brown Volvo with tan interior). My dad said something crazy like, "If you're not ready to go, do you want me to drive over to Nana's and come back and pick you up?"

"Oh, heck no!" I said to myself, "I'm going to choke Gary." I was moving fast because I was trying so hard to fix the peach cobbler my mother wanted for her birthday. My dad was waiting all day for this visit. He was so funny, just like a kid with a new toy. I really did not know this could very well be his grand entrance. To drive would make him feel like he really accomplished something big. Gary said he would meet us there.

He didn't want to drive in the car with us. Everybody knows when you get a license you need more experience.

My father knew that, but besides the fact he just got his license, he had never driven before and this was going to be a potential problem. My father was not willing to listen to me or anybody else. He was determined. Because he had taken the lessons and had the license, he felt he could do it. That was not the case though. He needed to have some experience. Besides that, he did not have a car. I decided he wanted to impress my mother on her birthday so that's why I was willing to let him drive.

How do you gently deal with an ego that has been so fragile? I discovered you must be honest on every level so here we go. "Dad," I said, "I'll be ready in 15 minutes. Is that alright?" He answered, "That will be fine." So I packed up the cobbler and out the door, we went with prayer on my lips. Believe me, my prayer was one of thanksgiving not one of fear: "Thank you, Father for the safe journey, and the peace and the joy that this will bring my father, in Jesus name Amen!"

I was so excited for him. I had decided if he had any questions he would ask me. He did well, except when it came to the stopping and turn signals. You know you cannot drive 25 miles per hour around the corners but that was not the time to aggravate him. I'd make suggestions later. "Whew!" "Dad, turn here," I said quickly, (I was trying to fix my wig because it shifted during the excitement as he turned the corner). It was the last corner before my mom's house. "Pull in the driveway," I said. We got out of the car and went in the house.

We were the first ones there. My father rang the bell. Mom answered and we all exchanged hellos and said happy birthday. My father was carrying the peach cobbler and he took it to the kitchen. My mom as of yet hadn't noticed that my father was driving.

I pulled her to the side and said in a whisper, "Ask dad if he has something to tell you."

My Father came into the living room where we were and said, "So, Mary, how is your birthday coming along?"

My mother said, "So far so good. But Toni says you have something to tell me."

He looked at me and said with a half smile, "You need to be quiet."

"So what is it William?" Mom asked.

"I got my driver's license yesterday, and I drove here today."

He was real calm and I was just trying to help him out. He thought she may have seen him drive up but she didn't. He didn't know how to bring it up so I did.

"Really!" she said.

"Yeah."

Three questions came out at once "What? When? How?"

As he began to tell the story, I left the room. I started talking to my grandmother. My mother's birthday turned out to be full of fun. Family and friends showed up. My father was smiling and everyone knew, by the time we left that night, he was now a licensed driver. We were all proud of his accomplishment.

Chapter Eight

TIME

The formless takes form in what we call "time." This is when a sequence of events moves into wholeness. It is a form of becoming. What we now see has come from that which we did not see. What is all this?

"Spirit *in motion*."

If it is Spirit then it is life. We are the seed ready to explode with potential and waiting for the timing and the Son. There is no way we can separate life from living. We have been taught there is no difference but there is.

We have the ability to withdraw from the source of all power that will cause us to express His image. What actually happened when Jesus walked through the crowd and was not able to be touched? He was spiritualized. Deep isn't it? I've learned as we come into the spiritual realm, which is natural and normal, *and* that we have to come into it, in its own nature. This is how Jesus put it:

Therefore, if thou bring thy gift to the altar, and there rememberest that thy brother hath ought against thee, leave there thy gift before the altar and go thy way; first be reconciled to thy brother and then come and offer thy gift

(Matthew 5:23-24)

Why?

Because you cannot enter into peace while you are in a state of confusion. You cannot manifest love with hate in your heart. (Ernest Holmes)

This is very important to understand because you can only have what you can take. We have not been conditioned to know that the same prayer answers the big and the small.

Nothing you can dream of is too great for you to undertake. The reason why we've become tired during the process of time is because some believe in the duality of good and evil. When in reality it's all good!

There is only one God and beside him, there is no other. God wants us to understand how to speak to ourselves. "Talk to yourself. Go within or do with out." (Bishop Jordan) TIME is a place in which you stand representing the truth. Your sight gets twisted when you are not focused. Don't abandon the word of God in the face of your adversity because it will do what He said it will do.

God is not becoming. God is. God is not growing. He is complete. God is not trying to find out something. God already knows. (Ernest Holmes)

We have only to open the portals of our soul and accept that which the Father has for us. We are unfolding to a discovery of our true nature. Man's nature is the same as God's nature. It's the Father's pleasure to give us the keys to the kingdom. With this in mind: We should learn how to receive the keys and use the keys and enjoy its full benefits.

We should be very careful so that when we are abstracting a Principle we do not forget the Essence. (Don't lose site of intimacy). Our soul ascends towards the knowledge of God. It only knows to do, it doesn't know why, it just does.

"Ice Water Wet"…"The soul is a doer or executer of the will of the spirit and has no choice of its own. It is the business of the soul to reflect the images that the spirit casts into it. Don't think of the soul and the spirit as being separate from each other because they are really two aspects of the same thing. The two are self-existent and co-eternal with the other. The soul has the power to produce and it receives all of the ideas that are given to it. If it could choose, it could reject. The spirit and the soul are eternal. They were never created. Only the body

This lesson is dedicated to that Truth which frees man from himself and sets him on the pathway of a new experience, which enables him to see through the mist to the Eternal and the Changeless Reality." (Ernest Holmes)

Chapter Nine

CALM TRUST

My father knew that he was now faced with something deep within himself. He wanted to remarry my mother. Everything he had held inside was staring him in the face; it became a Face book. It was an image of a dream that wanted to live and have a voice. Yes, those dead dreams wanted to live. All through the years, he had the lack of expression and it only brought him depression. Now it had ran ahead to the future to wait for him to awaken and make his vision plain. With every deliberate action, he was screaming, "I want my life back!" Well, here it is…

The path is plain and the word of God came through. I heard it defined like this: The word of God is Unremitting: what does that really mean? It demands hunger (*Mathew 5:6*). Continuing in time and space with out interruption…A Continuous Rearrangement.

The word is never slacking. It is ceaseless, continual, eternal, endless, persistent, constant, and timeless, round the clock, everlasting, nonstop, unending, and uninterrupted. To me this was very powerful to understand. At the end of November in 1999, William Holmes asked my mother to marry him. This was a place of decision. Exercising the power of choice, she said yes.

He apprehended the moment and it was the appointed time. What a redemption plan. It was a possible path but it wasn't easy and yet the path was ordered. The mental attitude is always important when you are manifesting a belief. Why is that, some may say? It is because false ideas of life must be uncovered and replaced by the truth. If it doesn't happen then, there is no freedom. We must erase any idea of failure. This is a truth you tell yourself about the spirit in you.

Be persistent and hold it in place (the dream). Failure isn't a person, a place, or a thing. It is a false thought that has no truth in it. It is a belief in limitation that does not exist. There is no limit in God! Speak your belief in calm trust. See it, feel it, and know it! Be the instrument that life will flow through.

On December 10, 1999, there was a wedding and a dream lived. The years it took really does not matter because the dream is ready to live when you are ready to stand...Some dreams need to stay dead but that is between you and God. Your faith will rise in the day of challenge. All things do work together for good. My father was standing in a place where he is recognizing the Word as power. This word broke down every man made law and cast it out.

He was standing in the presence of good. Nothing could change it. There was no other belief that could hinder it. It could not be reversed. Out of chaos, there was harmony. We were all excited about the wedding day. Things were moving fast and things had to be prepared, and living arrangements had been made. My father was moving to town. After they got married, they got a place together, in Highland Park, New Jersey.

It was really therapeutic for my father because they were a step away from a beautiful park. They began a life together for the second time and reflected only on the now. For, the past was buried with the mistakes. There was no way anyone can drive while looking in the rearview mirror. Interestingly, my father's driving had become better and his confidence had gotten stronger. Troi was the only one willing to take a long drive with him. That was okay. As for my father, he could care less. He was driving.

Dad always wanted to drive to Newark and let everybody see him. No one ever thought he would ever rise but knowing all the time, he should have. Whether it was family or friends, he was a different man, to all who had an encounter with him. It was a time where God spoke for Himself. It was the Lord's doing and it was marvelous in our eyes. The place my father worked was no longer looking like him.

I was working in a local hospital and had a friend there who was head of a department. So, I inquired of the Lord, "What can I do?" I wanted my father to have a job that gave him dignity and peace; you know something that would give him a sense of respect. Thankfully, a door opened up for him. Favor was his portion. He had become a very vital part of the working system because of favor. What exactly is this favor working on your behalf? I understand it like this: Favor contradicts fact. To contradict means to boldly declare the opposite. And that's it! "Whatever the truth of you is, you must boldly declare it." (Bishop Jordan)

My father started working 40-60 hours a week and making things happen. He was there when I came to work and he was there when I left. It was a gift from God to see him in the night and morning. Our lives were filling up with many things. Especially with memories that came from a good place. My father had begun to do everything but sing. He wanted no part of that and did not want to discuss it. Wholeness is what is promised and wholeness is what he had received.

I began to see my father live. He had a new confidence and it was evident my parents were building a life together for the first time. Their time, focus, and attention were directed toward each other. My mom had to learn to trust again and he had to learn to be a leader worthy of trusting. This was their journey together but what I had noticed was that their faith was the center.

I remember when they went on a cruise…My father tried to act like it was a regular everyday experience. Because he was experiencing things for the first time, I had to pry out of him what he had experienced. After a while, I got the emotion and the excitement. He was ready to travel after that. My mother had a husband that wanted to experience everything even decorating the house, but no cooking.

His trips to his family and friends with his grandsons were his biggest chest buster. Newark was no longer a place he longed for. But like the man, Jesus pulled aside from the multitude to open, that man had to go back and tell what the Lord had done. This is critical for the one who had no voice or who never heard the voice of reason and purpose.

The people saw and they heard the man, (my father), that had been tarred and fettered, then loosed and in his right mind. He wanted to thank the many people who had shown him kindness.

Chapter Ten

DIP DEEPLY

I know what I've come to understand, I can now have. I had to find some way to collect my thoughts after all this time. My father bought my mother a new car and he was so excited. He went out and purchased a house full of furniture. He did most of the things he'd always wanted to do for my mother. They even took trips to the top of the mountains. My uncle Lloyd owns 24 acres in the Blue Ridge Mountains.

My father saw life in motion and he was in it this time with his eyes wide open. Nothing came easy but he reached and found that the grapes were sweet. Watching my father grow into a man of courage was a sight to see. Everything I was forced to release was replaced. "There is something to this Living Water," I thought to myself.

...Sir, thou hast nothing to draw with, and the well is deep: from whence then hast thou that living water?

(John 4:11)

The thirst was unquenchable at first, but then the more I thirsted the more I was given. It had become very clear to me that I needed to dip a little deeper in the well. A superficial drink would never do. My father had to dip deeply as well. This was an opportunity to see what it means to redeem the time. A chance to see how God restores the years that the cankerworm had destroyed.

There are many stories waiting to be told. You know the ones where God can be seen as He moves through a life. The prison system is where people are that have unformed purposes and it looks like a pile of trash from a distance. But can I tell you that there is treasure in that trash?

It is the job of the Spirit to seek and save that, which is lost. We look in the highways and byways and compel men to come. But they are abused when they get here. If they don't grow like we want them to, we lose patience. The truth of the matter is, "He that hungers and thirst shall be filled." If there is no thirst then there is no quenching. Then we are not being the salt of the earth. Salt makes one thirsty. This is a spirit principle.

The spirit life is what is real. So we must know the Laws of Thinking (Bishop Jordan). So remember we take only what we can understand. This is why people are perishing for lack of knowledge and no understanding. The prison has a revolving door and the church dreams without manifesting. There is no pie in the sky because:

The eyes of the LORD run to and fro throughout the whole earth, to show himself strong in the behalf of them whose heart is perfect toward him
(II Chronicles 16:9)

This is "maturity." If you are not a creator, then you become the creature. If you don't know who you are then, you will never know where you are going. My father had to assume a role he knew nothing about and he had never seen...The role of a man. He worked hard at changing the pattern of his old life and the negative image of his past. This could never be easy; it only needed to be a choice and the help came after the choice was made.

You were never meant to walk alone. That was never the plan of God. My father had cycles of bad choices and could not find his way out. When you cannot find your way out, "DIP DEEPER." We must learn to put pressure on the covenant. The Word will stand in the midst of any transformation. The metamorphosis takes place in succession. We are always changing into something by feeding our faith or our fears.

My passion for those in the prison system was always there. I started visiting the prison in 1978 with a local church and as the years went on, I continued visiting throughout the years. I've joined many different groups and visited many juvenile detention centers in different states and I've visited death row in different prisons and women's correctional facilities. Most of my experience has been in male prisons. My father never did like the idea but he knew I could handle myself.

He expressed to me that he was not going back not even to visit. That was okay with me because I never asked him to go with me anyway. However, I was compelled to go for 30 years. I met some very interesting men and women, through my journey. Their stories are not the same but their excuses were quite common.

What I walked away with was more than I could share at any one time. I met children of incarcerated individuals. I did a project with a shelter in Newark some time ago. I experienced a bruising of a people not yet washed in the Blood (they had a need for social connection and were being excluded). I was under the direction of a leader who gave the plan. We brought people to church as they were, and they were shunned.

So the following week I gathered everyone from my former church to give me clothes from their closet not hand-me down items or items that they had sat aside to throw away, but clothes, shoes, stockings, ties, suits, and etc (things that they'd wear, good things). We brought all the items of clothing and shoes up on Saturday morning to give away along with haircuts and makeovers for the women.

We came back Sunday morning and made sure everyone was ready to go. We gave them all a dollar to put in the offering and off we went down the street. We went in two by two. We sat in different places throughout the church. When the Pastor began to tell people to hug one another, they got genuine hugs. When it was time for offerings, they had a seed. They were invited to dinner after service (all Newcomers). This project proved to be successful and is still in place.

We then moved on to the next project, which consisted of having teen group sessions. In these, we actually allowed them to talk about things that bothered them. We would then begin to reach within them to find where the pain and anger they were having was coming from. We followed up by working with them to reposition their thoughts for different steps.

I've seen families reunited and marriages restored and some weren't but that is between them and God. Some things must be built from the ground up, not restored, (This statement takes understanding). *Mathew 21:19* shows that if some things are not willing to produce, they must be commanded to be withered away.

I once visited a prisoner on death row, as I had done before. He stood out to me because he was suppose to. We talked for a while about him, about family, and about his children, but God had a word for him. And the Lord made sure the message was hand delivered. The Spirit of the living God has never ceased to amaze me. "Truly there is not a spot where God is not." (Bishop Jordan)

The experiences with the children in detention centers caused my emotions to be tapped. Eventually, I moved beyond that. Some children had no direction; some children were without purpose, and even without love. Many had been pressured to perform and their attitudes had been calloused to keep from breaking, and I've seen a lot of mental illness. But God has a plan in store and it is soon to come forth.

There seems to be a setup in place for them to fail. But God's plan provides a way in and a way out. It is his pleasure to give you the keys. To release and unlock the dream that is within you.

My journey through the system might be over, as I have known it. Like the Phoenix, I rise out of the ashes to tell a story about the silent voices that have not been heard. Those who think their cries, prayers and whatever faith they have, has been amiss. NOT SO! The winds of change have come to you. Right where you are!

For God has many names and on your tongue in your language to speak it, say it, and proclaim it from the heart. With assurance, know that you can only have what you understand. So understanding has come this day to you so that you may be able to know who you are. No more hiding, The Soul is not chained and the Spirit is not bound.

Conceive this word by taking it into your mind. To conceive suggests the idea of grasping something, as thought; to apprehend by reason or imagination.

Chapter Eleven

GARDEN OF EDEN

My father found himself in the Garden of Eden. What do I mean by that? Some would say that this garden does not exist. Or does it? The Garden of Eden typifies or represents man's original state of perfection before he began to have experiences. The Tree of Knowledge means Life Principle, (*Spirit*), which can be used both ways. It bore the fruit of knowledge of two kinds of experiences (good and evil, freedom and limitation).

Man must choose which kind of fruit he will eat. Man chose to depart from God (*all that is good*), *in all his goodness,* and man alone must choose to return. God lets him alone because he is a free agent and may do what he wills with himself. When a man decides to return to his Father's House, he will find his Father is still there. This can be difficult to digest when your belief is in another place but there is a place in us that is never fooled.

A place the Creator has carved out for Himself and it has nothing to do with religion or a particular denomination. It has to do with that "Substance" we are made of. It is Eternal...We all walk in Grace which is givingness, of the Spirit to its creation. *I like that...Thank you Lord.*

We ultimately want to be in a place of willingness and obedience. So we may partake of the goodness of the land. My father was in a place where he knew the Kingdom of God was within. He was in agreement, (Spirit, Soul, and Body). There was harmony and the only thing we saw moving was Spirit. My father was a man of few words. His contemplation and reflection was deep. I saw the words on his face. I often wanted to ask him, "Dad, what are you thinking?" But when I started to ask, somehow I knew the answer.

He would look at his grandkids, his wife, and his kids and would not be able to talk. The promise has always been--when you seek, you shall find. My father wanted to spend his life giving back and never felt satisfied with what he was giving. I guess all this came with his fate. I saw truth in rotation. As truth rises, it looks at you to see if anything is out of balance, and if it is, you check yourself by the standard of the Word. Not by another's standard for all have come short.

My father was now wearing the best robe. The robe was like the one that was given to the Prodigal Son when he came to himself. Everyone get's this robe. This robe was very significant it was a seamless garment and it represented a state of complete unity. Just like the ring, .The robe is seamless and the ring is without beginning or end. It begins everywhere and ends nowhere. The fatted calf represents the abundance of God's love and providence (care, economy, management). Everything was in the house just as he left it.

My father only had to turn and go half way, because The Father saw him from a distance. When he turned to God, God turned to him. No matter how long we have been away, God has always been there. I understood it this way: no matter how long you're in the dark, when we remember and come to ourselves anything we need is in the house.

The entrance of thy words gives light; it gives understanding unto the simple

(Psalm 119:130)

What actually happened to the darkness when the light showed up? Where did it come from and where did it go? I'll just have to wait for that answer. We can also find ourselves in the position of the elder son that stayed home. He was puffed up with self-righteousness, conceited, and fuming with anger over his brother's party. When we have an intolerant attitude towards others who do not think as we think it is the attitude of the elder brother.

God knows as little about self-righteousness as he knows about evil. Both are faults the elder son had been living in. He was in the midst of plenty and never recognized it. He only needed to ask and could have had all that the Father had. Both sons were foolish but which one was more deluded (deceived in the mind or judgment- Ernest Holmes)

Somehow, my father's sister felt that he had forgotten about her or didn't need her any longer, that's what he told me. But that was not the case he was just standing in a grip that needed no assistance and to tamper with him at that time would have been to obstruct (Stop the operation he was going through).

The Father is calling for order. This is where things are so arranged and they're playing their proper parts. Anything other than that is out of concert or harmony. When there is harmony, there is victory. "Victory as I have been taught is won in the silence of one's own soul…when you turn to the Father within." (Ernest Holmes)

Some people want you to walk their walk. You cannot and you must not or you become the hindrance. Who wants to be in the way of what the Father is doing? When a person decides not to dance in the dark the light comes. Before you call, I will answer…That's my promise (Jesus).

Chapter Twelve

CRUCIBLE

A severe test, as of patience or belief, or trial (the act or process of testing, trying, or putting to the proof: a trial of one's faith.

The Laws of Thinking

I have come to understand that *I should always run to the rock that is higher than I.* As I stood still, frozen, numb something was revealed to me that was somehow not a surprise. It was heavy and weighty but God was going to finish what He had started. I did not know how the gift of Prophecy operated even though it was asleep in me. A gift peeking out in dreams, in visions and in testimonies of what had come to pass, even after I had long forgotten about it. Often appearing as things I did not want to see whether it was in my life or someone else's.

This gift was now rising up and opening. I asked God a question and He gave me the answer. Now I had to handle it spiritually. How do you handle spiritual things? Certainly not as you would carnal things. There must be a just weight (a balance). So, I petitioned the Lord: *Hide me...*

I have been taught that as you believe, a demand must be made on your supply. I am an heir to all that the Father has. My father was fighting a good fight of faith, and cancer showed up. I saw it, I smelled it, and I rebuked it...But when I inquired of the Lord, He showed me the entire picture and I shared a small part of it with my mother. Only the part that I could release did I share.

My father was assured he did not have to worry himself about us. Which really meant: use your energy to keep strong. That's what I learned working in the hospital. People who are standing in faith spend so much time and energy trying to keep their loved ones strong, that they collapse with weakness at night, when things are still and quiet.

The nurses say they had a restless night. My father fought a good fight of faith. The Lord is Faithful, especially in your periods of transition. When the time came a little closer, this is what the Father did for us…An in-house Hospice center that I have never heard of showed up. It was a place where my father could go with no more meds, needles, and stuff that did not work. That stuff only made his quality of life a blur. But it was his life.

I petitioned the Lord, "Hide my father." And He did. The doctor showed up the next morning. I mentioned that I didn't want him to be so groggy. My father didn't like feeling like that. I asked the doctor, what I could do to keep him comfortable.

The doctor said, "Well we don't know."

The doctor came back and said," Listen there is a place he can go to. It's private but I think we can get him in there in just a couple of weeks."

"In a couple of weeks? That won't do," I said. "It just won't do."

So I petitioned the Lord: and this is what happened. I heard, "Early in the morning…Early…Three more weeks". I knew it was God.

So, I called the doctor and said, "He only has three more weeks."

He said, "Well that just doesn't sound right. We'll talk about it."

"That won't do," I said adamantly.

The next morning the doctor moved with haste and by evening, my father was settled into his new place. It was an 8-bed facility. He had a queen size bed, fireplace, and a dining room for family to eat in when they visited. A living room with windows a nice view, and no more medicine of any kind. He was alert, laughing, and visiting with everyone that came to see him.

He had all his grandchildren there on the bed, in the chairs, and everywhere. Troi was a Bail Bondsman and a Bounty Hunter. So in between his cases, he would come to visit and that meant all hours of the night. Visitation was allowed 24/7.

One morning as I was combing my hair in the mirror because I was getting ready to go to work, I heard: "Do you want to be there?" I stared at my face because I knew the voice. I did not answer, but I knew time was near. I had decided to ignore that. The voice was within me not outside of me. There was nowhere to hide. So I decided to pack something for the weekend (it was Thursday). I was doing hair because at that time, I had my own business.

"When I finish doing hair on Friday," I said to myself, "I'll spend the weekend with my father." When I finished that Friday night it was about 1:30 am. I had my weekend bag in the car. When I came to a crossroad, my car stopped at a stand still, I sat there trying to figure out what was going on in the middle of the fork in the road at 1:30 in the morning. I heard again, "Do you want to be there?"

I said as I laid my head on the steering wheel. "No." I made a right, went home, and said I'll let him rest. I'll go first thing in the morning. My mom was there until midnight she knew I was coming so she left to get rest, but she felt it was her last time there. At 4:00 am, I got a call from my mom. "Your dad passed," she said.

I could not help but feel God was kind to me. He gave me a chance to say another goodbye. Life was what my father asked for and life is what he had (10 full satisfying years). I heard a song by India Arie and it reminded me of a vision I had when my father dropped his coat of skin. It is called "Ready for Love."

In that vision the soul fixed its eyes on a love that was so real and bidding that to stay would only cause a feeling of longing and wanting. The Lord is our Shepherd, we shall not want. So the soul says, "If you'll have me I want to come…Bid me….He never looked back…It was exactly 3 weeks.

I heard sweetly now unto Him who was able to keep me from falling…Tell the story."

"My joy was full"

"THE CRUCIBLE"…*he had passed the test.*

Appendix

FAQ

1. Is alcoholism a disease?

Yes, alcohol dependency is diagnosed as alcoholism and it is a disease. Alcohol dependence alters parts of the brain from its normal healthy state, and because of that, this is called disease.

2. What is the difference between alcohol dependence and alcohol abuse?

The drinking repertoire: drink-seeking behavior, tolerance, withdrawal, drinking to relieve or avoid withdrawal symptoms, subjective awareness of the compulsion to drink, and a return to drinking after a period of abstinence.

3. Can you inherit alcoholism?

Remember: Risk is not destiny. Just because alcoholism might to run in families doesn't mean that a child of an alcoholic parent will automatically become an alcoholic. Some people can develop alcohol dependency even though no one in their family has a drinking problem. It is important to know if someone is at risk, be fore they develop a problem

4. How can you tell if someone has a problem?

Answering the following four questions can help you find out if you or a loved one has a drinking problem:

- Have you ever felt you should cut down on your drinking?
- Have people annoyed you by criticizing your drinking?
- Have you ever felt bad or guilty about your drinking?
- Have you ever had a drink first thing in the morning to steady your nerves or to get rid of a hangover?

5. If an alcoholic is unwilling to get help, what can you do about it?

This can be a challenge. An alcoholic can't be forced to get help except under certain circumstances, such as a traffic violation or an arrest that results in court-ordered treatment. But you don't have to wait for someone to "hit rock bottom" to act. Many alcoholism treatment specialists suggest that you seek help and get support when trying to get an alcoholic to get treatment:

6. **How can I help**

Stop all "cover ups, Time your intervention, be specific, Get help. Call on a friend,

Get support. It is important to remember that you are not alone. Support groups offered in most communities include Al-Anon, which holds regular meetings for spouses and other significant adults in an alcoholic's life, and Alateen, which is geared to children of alcoholics. These groups help family members understand that they are not responsible for an alcoholic's drinking and that they need to take steps to take care of themselves, regardless of whether the alcoholic family member chooses to get help.

You can call the National Drug and Alcohol Treatment Referral Routing Service **(Center for Substance Abuse Treatment)** at 1-800-662-HELP (4357) for information about treatment programs in your local community and to speak to someone about an alcohol problem.

7. **Do you have a family history of Alcoholism: Are you at Risk?**

This booklet contains basic information for anyone who is concerned about a family history of alcoholism. It lists organizations that can help relatives or friends of alcoholics.

Get support:

You can call the National Drug and Alcohol Treatment Referral Routing Service (Center for Substance Abuse Treatment) at 1-800-662-HELP (4357) for information about treatment programs in your local community and to speak to someone about an alcohol problem.

It is important to remember that you are not alone. Support groups offered in most communities include Al-Anon, which holds regular meetings for spouses and other significant adults in an alcoholic's life, and Alateen, which is geared to children of alcoholics. These groups help family members understand that they are not responsible for an alcoholic's drinking and that they need to take steps to take care of themselves, regardless of whether the alcoholic family member chooses to get help.

8. What Are the Physical Signs of Addiction?

The physical signs of abuse or addiction can vary depending on the person and the drug being abused. In addition, each drug has short-term and long-term physical effects. For example, someone who abuses marijuana may have a chronic cough or worsening of asthmatic conditions. Stimulants like cocaine increase heart rate and blood pressure, whereas opioids like heroin may slow the heart rate and reduce respiration. *Reference: www.about.com: Alcoholism*

RED FLAGS: to look out for:

1. Drinking to Get Drunk
2. Increased Consumption with Increased tolerance for Alcohol
3. Blackouts/ Memory Loss
4. Passing Out
5. Drinking Becomes a Primary Activity
6. Drinking Alone
7. Personality Changes
8. Secretive Drinking
9. Inability to Quit or Cut Back –Just some things to look out for.

9. What can the families of alcoholics do?

A.A. is just for the person that has difficulties with alcohol, but two other fellowships can help their relatives.
One is Al-Anon Family Groups. The other is Alateen, for teenagers who have alcoholic parents
www.al-anon.alateen.org/

10. What's the difference between Al-Anon and Alateen:

Al-Anon and **Alateen** are international organizations jointly known as **Al-Anon Family Groups** with a membership of over half a million men, women, and teens, providing a twelve-step program of recovery for friends and family members of alcoholics. Al-Anon is for adults within the program whereas Alateen is for young people (ages 12 to 20).

Al-Anon was formed in 1951 by Lois Wilson, wife of Alcoholics Anonymous (Bill Wilson)

In Lois's Story, she explained why, as the spouse of an alcoholic, she also required treatment. After a while, I began to wonder why I was not as happy as I ought to be, since the one thing I had been yearning for all my married life [Bill's sobriety] had come to pass. (Wikipedia)

11. What is Narcotics Anonymous (NA)?

NARCOTICS ANONYMOUS is also known as (NA) Drug addiction is widely considered a pathological state, which means: a condition that is not normal. Narcotics Anonymous sprang from the Alcoholics Anonymous Program of the late 1940s, with meetings first emerging in the Los Angeles area of California, USA, in the early Fifties. The NA program started as a small US movement that has grown into one of the world's oldest and largest organizations of its type.

12. Do I have to be using a specific drug to join NA?

Membership is open to all drug addicts, regardless of the particular drug or combination of drugs used. When adapting AA's First Step, the word "addiction" was substituted for "alcohol," thus removing drug-specific language and reflecting the "**disease** concept" of addiction

13. What can I expect if I join NA?

Recovering members share their successes and challenges in overcoming active addiction and living drug-free productive lives through the application of the principles contained within the Twelve Steps and Twelve Traditions of NA. These principles are the core of the Narcotics Anonymous recovery program. Principles incorporated within the steps include:

- Admitting there is a problem
- Seeking help
- Engaging in a thorough self-examination
- Confidential self-disclosure
- Making amends for harm done

NA describes itself as a nonprofit "fellowship or society of men and women for whom drugs had become a major problem," and it is the second-largest 12-step organization in existence.

Key Fact about NA:
"Ensuring that information is accessible only to those authorized to have access." Information, Security and Confidentiality is first and foremost.

14. What's the nature of addiction?

NA describes addiction as a progressive disease with no known cure, which affects every area of an addict's life: physical, mental, emotional, and spiritual. NA suggests that the disease of addiction can be arrested, and recovery is possible through the NA twelve-step program. The steps never mention drugs or drug use; rather they refer only to addiction, to indicate that addicts have a disease of which drug use is one symptom. Other symptoms include obsession, compulsion, denial, and self-centered fear: Reference *Wikipedia*

15. What is meant by a drug relapse?

Drug relapse is a frustrating problem for many trying to recover from drug or alcohol problems. Those who have problems with drugs or alcohol find themselves on a perpetual roller coaster that involves periods of abstinence, reduction of use, and relapse. Often times this is due to external factors such as the availability of drugs and societal pressures, anger / frustration and temptation.

The children: What about the children?

"Whoever receives a little child like this in my name receives me"
(International standard version)

- Nearly 2 million children in the US under 18 have a parent in prison.

- 58% of men in N.Y. state prisons are Fathers and 72% of women incarcerated are Mothers.

- 1 in 40 children in the US has a parent in prison

- More than 650,000 people will leave state and federal prisons this year, most returning to the low income, urban communities they left.

- Spouses of alcoholics wait, on average, seven years before making an intervention."

- Alcohol problems occur at different levels of severity, from mild and annoying to life threatening.

Incarceration: Oftentimes, children experience shame and isolation, and they are stigmatized by the larger society. They feel guilty and are unsure if they are to blame for their parents. Children have varying reactions to the trauma of separation from a parent due to incarceration. In addition, children may feel extreme sadness and anger toward their parents or toward the authority that removed them.

When children feel unsafe or begin to interpret the world as unpredictable, they can experience high levels of anxiety, which can result in depression, aggressive behavior or other forms of acting out.

Without support and services for these children, they are at risk of repeating the behavior of their parents or becoming incarcerated themselves. The intergenerational cycle of crime and incarceration—a cycle that leaves children with incarcerated parents more likely to be incarcerated as adults

TVCP (Tele-Visitation for Children of Prisoners)
TVCN EFFECT NOW by the PB&J (network) PEANUT BUTTER AND JELLY NETWORK

TVCP is an innovative program created to strengthen relationships between children and their incarcerated parents, particularly when contact visits are not feasible for families. Using televideo conferencing equipment in their own communities, youth are able to visit their inmate parents on a regular basis. Families are assessed for case management and therapeutic needs and are provided with support throughout the visitation process, setting the stage for successful reintegration, after prison.

Tele-Visitation for Children of Prisoners Location:
PB&J Family Services, Inc.
Administrative Offices and
Peanut Butter & Jelly Therapeutic Preschool
1101 Lopez Rd. SW
Albuquerque, NM 87105
Phone: (505) 877-7060

If interested in videophone visits please visit this web site: http://pbjfamilyservices.org
Or contact: toniholmesthebookwriter@gmail.com

Bill of Rights

This **Bill of Rights** was also published in the Report of the Blue Ribbon Commission on the Welfare of Children of Jailed and Incarcerated Parents, authorized under New Mexico Executive Order 2006-022; November 1, 2006.

1. I have the right to be kept safe and informed at the time of my parent's arrest.

2. I have the right to be heard when decisions are being made about me.

3. I have the right to be considered when decisions are being made about my parent.

4. I have the right to be well cared for in my parent's absence.

5. I have the right to speak with, see, and touch my parent.

6. I have the right to support as I face my parent's incarceration.

7. I have the right not to be judged, blamed, or labeled because my parent is incarcerated.

8. I have the right to a life-long relationship with my parent.

NEWMEXICOCITIZEn

Help Lines:

N.J. Statewide Help Line
1-800-992-0401

Central Jersey Area Service Committee
Narcotics Anonymous
Call for Meetings & Information

Help Lines in other areas:

Alcohol and Drug 24 hour Hotline
1-800-252-6465

Alcohol and Drug Referral Hotline
1-800-252-6465

Cocaine 24 hour Help Line
800-COCAINE (800-262-2463)

National Runaway Switchboard and Suicide Hotline
1-800-621-4000

Tough Love International
1-800-333-1069

American Council for Drug Education
1-800-488-3784

Nar-Anon Family Groups
1-800-477-6291

National Association for Children of Alcoholics
1-888-554-2627

National Coalition of Hispanic Health and Human Services Organizations
1-800-504-7081

National Inhalant Prevention Coalition
1-800-269-4237

FREEVIBE.com

Is an informative web site that will help parents and loved ones understand the effects of illegal drugs, it will give you facts and information. This website keeps it real and exact. Anything you need to know even concerning what to do if you know someone who needs help. What to say, and expert advice, on what to do: Such as, does your friend have a drug problem? Or drug scenarios.
This site gives Yellow flag information –pre-help and Red flag information-during and post help.

The Children of Promise, NYC

Embracing and empowering children of incarcerated parents

600 Lafayette Avenue, 6th Floor

Brooklyn, NY 11216

(718) 483-9290

This is an organization that is close to my heart, consider being a mentor and please be generous in your support and in your giving to them. Thank You

REFERENCES

Helpful Books:

Hasin, D.S.; Grant, B.; & Endicott, J. The natural history of alcohol abuse: Implications for definitions of alcohol use disorders.

Wilson, Lois (1995). "Lois's Story," *How Al-Anon Works for Families and Friends of Alcoholics*. Virginia Beach, Virginia: Al-Anon Family Group Headquarters, Inc., 136-137. ISBN 0910034265. OCLC 32951492.

Scripture References for further reading:

The Lord upholdeth all that fall: and raiseth up all those that be bowed down.

(Psalms 145:14)

And again he said to me, be a Prophet to these bones, and say to them oh dry bones, Give ear to the word of the Lord.

(Ezekiel 37:4)

And when he came to himself, he said, How many hired servants of my fathers have bread enough and to spare, and I perish with hunger.

(Luke 15:17)

... that whatsoever ye shall ask of the <u>Father</u> in my name, he may give it you

(John 15:16)

And they said among themselves, who shall roll away the stone from the door of the Sepulcher?

(Mark 16:3)

For the heart of this people is waxed gross, and their ears are dull of hearing, and their eyes have they closed; lest they should see with their eyes, and hear with their ears, and understand with their heart, and should be converted, and I should heal them.

(Acts 28:27)

...Awake thou that sleepest, and arise from the dead, and Christ shall give thee light.

(Ephesians: 5:14)

I and my Father are one

(John 10:30)

Let this mind be in you, which was also in Christ Jesus

(Philippians 2:5)

He went out, bearing his cross, to the place called the place of the skull, which is called in Hebrew Golgotha.

(John: 19:17)

The eyes of your understanding being enlightened

(Ephesians 1:18)

...Sir, thou hast nothing to draw with, and the well is deep: from whence then hast thou that living water?

(John 4:11)

My people are destroyed for lack of knowledge.

(Hosea 4:6a)

All things work together for good.

(Romans 8:28)

About the Author

Toni Holmes: is a graduate of *"University of Medicine & Dentistry of New Jersey / Institute For Chemical Dependency"* where she earned a degree in *Biopsychosocial Assessment, Diagnosis, Crisis Intervention with alcohol and drug clients, Treatment strategies with children in dysfunctional Families, Group counseling with alcohol and drug clients, Community Resources for domestic Violence Case, and Dimensions of recovery.*

Toni has worked in New Brunswick as a sworn in probation officer and as a fully armed Bounty Hunter in Middlesex and surrounding counties. She has been a volunteer prison counselor since 1977. She is also an ordained Prophetess in the established order "P.O.M.E." (Prophetic Order of Mar Elijah). Toni's passion is speaking life into the lives of others.

www.ingramcontent.com/pod-product-compliance
Lightning Source LLC
Chambersburg PA
CBHW032048090426
42744CB00004B/124